Second Thoughts about Hell

An online resource to help preachers engage the notion of hell in the pulpit is available at **www.wjkbooks.com/Hell**. The resource includes a general orientation to the subject and suggestions for sermon series based on biblical texts and topics.

"What an informative, readable, and well-conceived book! Ronald Allen and Robert Cornwall offer brief summaries of how biblical writers, early Christians, major theologians, and contemporary scholars think about hell. And they do so in a lively way. Allen and Cornwall even reveal their own views at the end. This is a great book for small group discussions!"
    —Thomas Jay Oord, author of *God Can't: How to Believe in God and Love after Tragedy, Abuse, and Other Evils*

"*Second Thoughts about Hell* is an informative, thought-provoking, and accessible read. Tackling a topic many avoid, this book explores the concept of hell through historical, biblical, Protestant, and modern lenses. Ideal for study groups and faith communities, it includes a comprehensive study guide that encourages deeper reflection and discussion. A valuable resource for anyone wanting to engage seriously with one of theology's most challenging subjects."
    —Grace Ji-Sun Kim, Professor of Theology, Earlham School of Religion, and author of *Earthbound*, *When God Became White*, and *Invisible*

"Allen and Cornwall describe historical and contemporary understandings of the afterlife, deftly demonstrating how social/cultural contexts inadvertently invite the church to embrace one understanding over another. But this volume is not simply an academic, ivory tower exploration. The authors know that what we believe about last things, about heaven and hell, strongly inform our understandings of the mission of the church, the purposes of worship and preaching, and the ways we provide care and hope to our congregations and wider communities. It is a very important conversation. (Or we might say a hell of a conversation.)"
    — Mary Donovan Turner, Professor Emerita of Preaching, Pacific School of Religion

"When people say, 'Go to hell,' few know more than it is not a nice place. I love this book, which could be titled *Everything You Want to Know about Hell but Were Afraid to Ask*. What happens after we die? Is hell real? What does it have to do with God? In clear, simple language, Allen and Cornwall faithfully review what

the Bible and theologians through the ages have said, opening a surprising range of possibilities for readers to consider. No study is more helpful than this for both preachers and laypeople in seeking answers."
—Paul Scott Wilson, Professor Emeritus of Homiletics, Emmanuel College of Victoria University in the University of Toronto

"Anyone who has had second thoughts about hell will appreciate Allen and Cornwall's efforts in this book to help us understand better what we believe about this and why. They have done their homework (on a vast literature), written clearly and succinctly (on difficult associated concepts), and treated a full range of views charitably and yet without avoiding the critical questions from other perspectives. If *Second Thoughts about Hell* does not prod you to change your mind, it will at least equip those with pastoral and teaching responsibilities to engage and also facilitate important conversations about a Christian doctrine with deep roots in the theological tradition."
—Amos Yong, Chief Academic Officer, Dean of the School of Mission and Theology, and Professor of Theology and Mission, Fuller Theological Seminary

"In *Second Thoughts about Hell,* authors Allen and Cornwall guide readers on a journey of understandings of hell in the Bible, the history of the church, and more recent theological reflection. They helpfully summarize the major views of hell today, from a literal hell to universal salvation, advocating for an understanding of hell that supports rather than undermines a life-affirming, hope-filled depiction of God and the human future. Readers will appreciate the book's clarity and the authenticity with which the authors share, but do not impose, their own beliefs. A study guide for small groups and web-accessible suggestions for both topical and lectionary-based sermon series accompany the book."
—Alyce M. McKenzie, Le Van Professor of Preaching and Worship and Altshuler Distinguished Teaching Professor, Perkins School of Theology, SMU, and codirector, The Perkins Center for Preaching Excellence, SMU

Second Thoughts about Hell

Understanding What We Believe

Ronald J. Allen
Robert D. Cornwall

© 2024 Ronald J. Allen and Robert D. Cornwall

First edition
Published by Westminster John Knox Press
Louisville, Kentucky

25 26 27 28 29 30 31 32 33 34—10 9 8 7 6 5 4 3 2 1

All rights reserved. No part of this book may be reproduced or transmitted in any form or by any means, electronic or mechanical, including photocopying, recording, or by any information storage or retrieval system, without permission in writing from the publisher. For information, address Westminster John Knox Press, 100 Witherspoon Street, Louisville, Kentucky 40202-1396. Or contact us online at www.wjkbooks.com.

Unless otherwise indicated, Scripture quotations are taken from the New Revised Standard Version Updated Edition. Copyright ©2021 National Council of Churches of Christ in the United States of America. Used by permission. All rights reserved worldwide.

Book design by Sharon Adams
Cover design by designpointinc.com

Library of Congress Cataloging-in-Publication Data is on file
at the Library of Congress, Washington, DC.

ISBN: 978-0-664-26906-7 (paperback)
ISBN: 978-1-646-98434-3 (ebook)

Most Westminster John Knox Press books are available at special quantity discounts when purchased in bulk by corporations, organizations, and special-interest groups. For more information, please email SpecialSales@wjkbooks.com.

Contents

Acknowledgments	vii
Introduction	1

Part One: Voices on Hell from the World of the Bible   17
1. Voices from the Old Testament   19
2. Voices from Early Judaism   26
3. Voices from the New Testament   35

Part Two: Voices on Hell from the History of the Church   57
4. Voices from the Second Century CE to the Reformation   59
5. Voices from the Reformation to the Twentieth Century   73

Part Three: Voices Nuancing the Discussion about Hell   89
6. Voices from the Roman Catholic Church   91
7. Voices from the Modern Worldview: Bultmann and Tillich   99
8. Voices Reclaiming Revelation: Barth, Brunner, and the Postliberals   107
9. Voices of Eschatological Theologians: Käsemann, Moltmann, and Pannenberg   117
10. Voices from Liberation Theology   124
11. Voices from Open and Relational Theologies   130

vi   Contents

Part Four: Voices Summarizing Three Main Views of Hell Today   137
12. Voices on a Literal Hell That Continues Forever   139
13. Voices on Annihilationism: An Alternative to Continuous Punishment in Fire   143
14. Voices on Universal Salvation   147

Afterword   153
    What Does Ron Believe?   153
    What Does Bob Believe?   158

Study Guide   163
    Session One: Introductory Matters and Voices from the Bible   165
    Session Two: Voices in Christian Tradition   168
    Session Three: Roman Catholic Voices   171
    Session Four: Voices from the Contemporary World   172
    Session Five: Three Viewpoints: Eternal Punishment, Annhilationism (Conditionalism), and Universal Salvation   175
    A Final Word   177

Notes   179
Suggestions for Further Reading   191

Acknowledgments

Just a few years ago, neither Ron nor Bob would have thought they would write a book about hell. However, it is a topic of great concern, especially among Christians who find traditional teachings about the topic to be at best disconcerting, if not a reason to abandon the faith. As is true with our previous book, *Second Thoughts about the Second Coming,* we thought we could help those concerned about this concept that has played such a central role in Christian thought and practice by offering a guide to the biblical, historical, and contemporary views of hell, allowing for conversations to take place that, hopefully, can strengthen people's faith.

We want to begin by thanking the entire Westminster John Knox Press team for agreeing to publish a sequel to our previous book on the second coming and the afterlife. We are greatly pleased with that first book and the strong response given to it by readers. Now, with this second book, we want to start by thanking our original editor, David Dobson, who continually encouraged us in the writing process, letting us know we were on the right track. Stacy Davis later inherited our project and provided excellent guidance and support in helping bring the book to completion. Then there is the rest of the team who have supported our project, including Natalie Smith, who served as our publicist on the first book and is doing so again with this book. It has been a great joy for both of us to work with the team at Westminster John Knox Press.

Beyond the support and guidance given by the team at WJK, several other people have contributed in one way or another to the success of this project. We would like to thank Ron Greene, Brett Cornwall, Monica Mitri, and Keith Huey for their readings of all or parts of the book and their guidance regarding what we had written. Terry Bradbury, a lay member of Central Christian Church (Disciples of Christ) in Indianapolis, provided Ron with numerous news items illustrating the presence of hell in contemporary conversations. Bob would like to thank Chad Bahl for permitting him to draw on Bob's chapter "To Hell and Back: A History of Hell," published as part of *Deconstructing Hell: Open and Relational Responses to the Doctrine of Eternal Conscious Torment,* edited by Chad Bahl (SacraSage Press, 2023).

This has been a most enjoyable writing partnership for both of us. However, we couldn't do this without our spouses' support, encouragement, and general understanding that both of us have a compulsion to write. With that in mind, we wish to give thanks to our spouses, Linda McKiernan-Allen and Cheryl Cornwall.

Finally, as with our first book, we have written this book for the church that we have both served through the years. We thank God for the opportunity to use the gift of writing in service to the church. May this book, as was *Second Thoughts about the Second Coming,* be received as a gift to the church at large and in honor of the God we serve in Jesus Christ.

Blessings,
Bob Cornwall and Ron Allen
Advent 2024

Introduction

This book came about in the same way as our earlier *Second Thoughts about the Second Coming*. We became aware of a question put to us in many Bible study groups in congregations in which we have been guest leaders in the long-established denominations. The question is some form of "what can we Christians believe about hell?" Most of the time, this question seems to come from an honest curiosity. People are exposed to popular ideas about hell in conversation and on the internet and wonder what to make of them. Even seasoned Bible students are often influenced in their perceptions of hell more by the excruciating pictures in Dante's *The Divine Comedy* or John Bunyan's *The Pilgrim's Progress* than by the more limited images of hell in the Bible. Often, the question comes from a deep struggle over whether a God "abounding in steadfast love" (Exod 34:6–7) would condemn people to an eternity of punishment, whether by fire or by some other means.

At other times, a participant's question comes from a difficult personal background. "My father was an alcoholic who abused his family and left us destitute. Is he burning in hell right now?" Sometimes the question is asked in the frame of social justice. Referring to a person or group who caused others to suffer, someone said, "I want to know that those who did wrong to so many will get what they deserve." If the questioner has a somewhat conservative religious orientation, the question is sometimes a little suspicious, as if the participant is thinking, "We've heard about liberal ministers who do not believe the Bible. Are you one of those?" If the questioner has a progressive religious orientation, the question is often suspicious in a dismissive way. "I have decided that a God of love would not tolerate a fiery hell. You are committed to the Bible. Does that mean you are committed to the idea of hell?" Then there is the question of freedom of choice. C. S. Lewis, in *The Great Divorce*, writes, "Any [person] may choose eternal death. Those who choose it will have it."[1] Well, is that true?

Some of our progressive friends, when hearing about this project, seemed bemused. "Who is interested in hell these days?" While that may be the case in many progressive orbits, we continue to see articles about hell in the news. One of Ron's friends sent him several newspaper, magazine, and online articles about hell from respectable sources that were published in 2024 as we were working on the book.

Along the way, a discussion often ensues in a study group or other setting in which participants put forward their differing views on what hell may be and how people might experience it. For example:

- Hell is a literal place of blistering punishment.
- Hell is a "refiner's fire" purifying the self from the effects of sin (often similar to the Roman Catholic doctrine of purgatory).
- Hell is alienation from God and others in the present and/or in the future.
- Hell is annihilation (the consciousness of the human being disappears).
- Hell does not exist because a loving God will not punish people in the ways associated with hell (e.g., an eternity of fire) and will ultimately save everyone (universal salvation).

This list is only representative of a much wider field of interpretations. In the study guide at the end of this volume, we invite readers to add to this list their own associations with hell and other interpretations they have heard.

The Meaning of "Hell" in This Book

Over the years, we (Bob and Ron) have noticed that church groups sometimes get into discussions without being clear regarding what the discussion is about. Hence, we pause for clarification. In this book, we follow the definition offered by Alan Bernstein, who speaks of hell as "a divinely sanctioned place of eternal torment for the wicked. It is 'divinely sanctioned' because the God (or, the gods) who established it could have refrained from creating it and could at any time demolish it. Its existence depends on some divinely established purpose."[2] The first thing that often comes to mind when we think of hell is an underworld of fire and brimstone where people suffer for eternity. However, we will see later in the book that this is not the only way in which hell is pictured in the Bible and other Jewish and Christian writings.

We say that hell is an ongoing form of punishment, usually in the afterlife, to distinguish it from singular acts of punishment that God metes out for a limited duration and that typically take place in this life. Revelation 20:10 is an example of the popular view of hell as eternal punishment: God throws the devil into the lake of fire to join the beast and the false prophet in being "tormented day and night forever and ever." There is no release from this fire. As an example of an act of singular punishment, we note that Second Isaiah declares that God had acted through the Babylonians to punish Judah for its idolatry and concomitant sins by sending the leaders of Judah into exile (e.g., Isa 43:27–28). In two generations, according to Isaiah, God released the Judahites from exile and returned them to their own land, using Cyrus the Persian (e.g., Isa 45:1). The exile, while painful and lasting two generations, was nonetheless a limited event.

To be sure, in Jewish and Christian history and theology, hell as eternal punishment in the afterlife and judgment as a singular event are not hard-and-fast categories, nor are they exhaustive. We concentrate on views of hell in the Bible and Christian traditions. Other religious traditions have views of harsh things that take place after death, but such traditions lie beyond the scope of this book.

Uses of the Word "Hell"

We begin with a definition because the word "hell" is used in so many ways. One of the most common uses of "hell" is as a general expression for suffering, as when a person is in a painful health crisis and says, "I am going through hell." Strictly speaking, according to the understanding of hell set out above, that statement would mean that the person believes God sent the illness as a punishment. However, most theologies today would say that this expression is technically incorrect. God does not visit sickness upon people to punish them. Illness occurs when parts of the body malfunction.

People use the word "hell" in many other ways. It sometimes functions as an expletive, as in "Damn it to hell!," "Hell, yes!," or "Oh hell!" It can mean "really good" as in "That was a hell of a sermon." In situations in which people disagree, it sometimes has a disparaging character, as in "To hell with it" or "Oh, go to hell." A person does something "for the hell of it," meaning just for the fun of it. Someone who "catches hell" is being severely criticized. A minister might think of a particular pastorate as "a long time in hell." Someone memorably said, "Hell is a hell of a thing to think about."

While we explore many different interpretations of hell in this volume, it is important to remember that when we speak of hell, we tend to have in mind God punishing people for long time periods, typically in the afterlife. At the same time, readers need to be alert to the specific associations with hell (and broader views of punishment) in particular passages in the Bible and Christian history and theology.

This Book Offers a Wide Range of Possibilities

Our purpose with this book is not to persuade readers that hell exists or does not exist. Nor do we try to lead the reader to a particular understanding of hell. Rather, we set out different views of hell in the Bible, Christian history, and Christian theology, including the idea that there is no hell and that God does not directly punish individuals or communities. We try to describe the viewpoints clearly, succinctly, and respectfully. We hope that those who hold the views we depict will recognize what they really think and not feel put down, dismissed, or disrespected. Along the way, we identify what we see as strengths and weaknesses in these views.

In the end, we hope readers will be able to identify the perspective(s) that make the most sense to them given what they believe about God and the world and why they believe what they believe. We further hope that study groups using the book will become communities of respectful conversation as people come to better understand one another on the journey to clarification.

Why Devote a Book to the Topic of Hell?

Some friends point out that in the strict sense, we cannot *know* whether there is a hell in the sense of God invoking long-lasting punishment, so why worry about it now? What is the point of thinking about what Christians believe about hell in an epoch of history marked by so many tensions in matters of race and ethnicity, sexuality and gender, ecology, political polarization, and economic uncertainty, not to mention violence? With so many experiences and issues of immediate existential importance in the present moment, it is not surprising that many people are disinterested in hell.

This disinterest extends not only to many laypeople but also to many clergy. We recently led a workshop on our book *Second Thoughts about the Second Coming* for preachers and asked, "How many of you preach at least once in a while on the second coming?" Only one hand went up. The others replied with variations on the remark, "There is so much happening *now* that I really feel I need to address that."

We offer a threefold response. First, we hope the book helps readers come to greater clarity regarding the place of hell in Christian witness. The mission of the church is to witness to what it most deeply believes to be true about God, God's purposes for the world, and appropriate responses. To oversimplify, we may say that from the time of the writing of the last twenty-seven books of the Bible to the present, many Christians and many churches have believed that while God's intent to save is God's primary purpose, hell awaits those who disobey God's purposes.

- If a Christian or a congregation or Christian movement continues to believe that God will condemn the unfaithful to hell—whether imagining hell as a burning pit in which the fire never goes out or in some other form—then that community is morally obligated to make it a part of their witness. They need to alert people to the possibility of hell as a final destination and invite people to take steps to avoid hell.
- If a Christian or a congregation or a Christian movement believes that disastrous consequences of a singular event of punishment can come because of disobedience—whether God directly causes those consequences or people bring the consequences on themselves—they are morally obligated to make that belief clear so that others have opportunities to choose to live more faithfully and to avoid the consequences.
- If a Christian or a congregation or a Christian movement does not believe that hell awaits, they too are obligated to clarify their position to relieve others of the unnecessary anxiety of the fear of hell, anxiety that often siphons off energy that could go into fuller living toward God's positive purposes for humankind and nature.

The integrity of the Christian witness is at stake. We need to say what we believe and believe what we say, and we need to live accordingly.

Second, many individuals and congregations in the long-established churches are uncertain about what they believe about hell because they have inadequate data to make informed choices. Preaching and teaching in these churches have given little overt attention to the notion of hell over the last generations. As a result, many people are left to think about hell based on little more than images of hell in popular media and references to hell in folk theology that are passed from person to person without serious interaction with the Bible or Christian history and theology.

Ron remembers a conversation among progressive and moderate ministers that drifted into the subject of hell. After a few humorous interchanges about hell, one of the ministers said flatly, "I don't preach about hell because I don't care about it. I care about what is happening now." While this preacher may not care about it, our impression is that some laypeople in the long-established churches do care about it (per our report from our Bible study experiences above) and would welcome responsible guidance.

Our inkling is that many evangelical churches are clear in believing that there is a hell and that people should accept God's grace and live in such a way as to avoid landing there. Our impression is also that many evangelical preachers today go lightly on "fire and brimstone" sermons and take more reasoned approaches to hell. However, our further inkling is that such congregations are seldom exposed to the wider range of responsible interpretations of hell, including arguments that hell does not exist.

A growing postevangelical movement has come to life in which many evangelicals express serious questions about whether they can continue to believe in hell, at least as popularly understood. Many of these people are aware of their doubts about hell, but they're not aware of resources that can help them reformulate their thinking about hell in ways that are appropriate to their freshly redeveloping deepest convictions about God. We believe this book, with its array of resources, will be of particular interest to the postevangelical movement.

Third, what we believe about hell has practical consequences for how we live in the present. For some, this means evangelizing friends, family, and neighbors, to make sure they don't end up in hell. For others, those who reject the idea of hell, there is sometimes the need to reinforce the idea that a God of love would not consign a person to an eternity of torment in hell. This message may draw some into the church, but it can also push them away. Among the reasons noted by many who leave behind Christianity is the message that the Christian God consigns people to eternal damnation if they do not become Christians (accept Jesus as savior). Many people are simply confused, believing that a God of love would not consign people to hell, and yet they are not sure there is another option. What this means for clergy is that these questions and concerns have a pastoral dimension, which we will take note of later in the book.

Words for Hell in the Bible

We will talk about this matter at important points in the book, but we mention it now so that readers can be alert to it. Different words in Hebrew and Greek lie behind the English translations that use "hell." In the older versions of the Bible, "hell" often translates the Hebrew word *sheol,* as in Psalm 139:8 in the King James Version: "If I ascend up into heaven, thou art there: if I make my bed in hell, behold, thou art there." Today's reader may think of hell in Psalm 139 (and many other places in the Old Testament) as the fiery place of punishment, whereas most of the time *sheol* refers in a much more neutral way to the underworld abode where the dead reside, without real suggestion of it being a place of punishment. Many of the more recent English versions simply use "Sheol."

In the New Testament, in both older and newer versions, the English term "hell" sometimes renders the Greek *hades* or *gehenna*. The word *hades* usually refers to an abode of the dead similar to *sheol*. But occasionally it seems to be a way of speaking about a place of punishment. While that word is sometimes translated as "hell," it is also sometimes transliterated as "Hades." (In transliteration, the writer simply uses comparable English letters for the letters in the original language.)

Similarly, the Greek *gehenna* is sometimes translated as "hell" and sometimes transliterated as "Gehenna." It is derived from the Hebrew name that means "Valley of Hinnom," a location near Jerusalem where child sacrifice occurred (2 Kgs 16:3; Jer 19:4–5) and where the Babylonians slaughtered many Judeans (Jer 7:29–34). In the Old Testament, this valley is infamous as a symbol of idolatrous and sinful behavior but is not associated with an afterlife. However, in the last centuries before the New Testament, several Jewish writings described the valley as a place of punishment. We explain this development in chapter 2.

Many other expressions in the New Testament also bespeak a place of punishment in the life beyond this one. Three examples illustrate the wide range of references to hell. We have already referred to "the lake of fire" (Rev 20:10). Matthew denotes hell when speaking of the place where there is weeping and gnashing of teeth (Matt 8:12; 13:42, 50; 22:13; 24:51; 25:30). Paul occasionally speaks of "perishing" as a way of indicating the final disposition of the unfaithful (e.g., 1 Cor 1:18).

Our point here is simply that the reader needs to consider which meaning of a word or phrase is at work in a particular passage. Of course, scholars and others can debate "which meaning of a word or phrase" is present in a particular passage.

A Two-Step Approach to Making Sense of What We Believe about Hell

Coming to a clear and well-founded understanding of hell requires two steps, which we preview here and draw on more fully as we approach different interpretations of hell as the book unfolds. The first step is to consider what sources ask readers to believe about hell in light of the historical, literary, and theological settings of the source. When studying the Bible, this work is sometimes called biblical exegesis. The second step is to consider whether we believe the same things that particular sources believe or whether we come to different beliefs. We make this second determination—what we believe—based on our deepest convictions about God.

The idea here is to honor the otherness, the distinctive characteristics, of a text in the Bible or a voice in Christian history. The ancient and not-so-ancient authors spoke and wrote at specific moments of history, addressed issues pertinent to their time, used language that had meanings particular to that moment, operated out of worldviews they took for granted, and did not envision speaking to people several centuries down the road. Their ideas can be quite different from ours. In the biblical period and for quite a while afterward, for instance, many people thought of the world as a three-story universe with heaven above, the earth in the middle, and an underworld below. They could speak literally of going "up" to heaven and "down" to hell.

Concerning the first step, we can often reconstruct what the biblical writers and sources meant when they spoke about hell. To be sure, scholars sometimes disagree about aspects of what an ancient source asked their hearers and readers to believe, but these disagreements take place under the umbrella of trying to reconstruct what the ancient "other" had in view. The key question is,

"What did a particular source ask readers or hearers to believe about hell in light of that source's context in history?" For example, what does the Gospel of Matthew intend when it speaks of "weeping and gnashing of teeth" (Matt 8:12; 13:42, 50; 22:13; 24:51; 25:30)?

Many Bible study groups attempt to follow this model. But uneasiness with certain biblical passages sometimes leads Christians to look for ways of interpreting the Bible that make them feel better but that do not honor the integrity of the text. When thinking about a particular passage in the Bible, we sometimes hear people say, "Well, my interpretation of this text is . . . ." and then put forward an idea that might be creative but is not something an ancient or not-so-ancient writer would have had in mind. For example, one person in a Bible study group, commenting on the reference to the lake of fire in Revelation 20:10, said, "Hell to me is just a state of mind of being aware of separation from God." To be sure, we need to consider the degree to which the verse in Revelation refers to literal fire or fire as a symbol, but to our knowledge, no responsible interpreter would say it refers only to a state of mind in the book of Revelation.

The second step in making sense of hell is to clarify what we believe about it. In a sense we carry out an exegesis of our process of coming to clarity, recognizing the different sources that come into play—and how we draw on them—in seeking to come to clarity: the Bible, voices from history, contemporary voices, our own experience, and the logic or reasoning by which we arrive at a particular interpretation. We bring what we discovered in step one into conversation with voices from history, tradition, reason, and experience as well as what we most deeply believe about God. A key question for all approaches is how to reconcile the notion that God acts in love and justice with beliefs about hell.

This can be a messy process, and if the experience of Bob and Ron is true for others, we are often tempted to default too quickly to a point of view that makes us feel better than some other viewpoints. For this reason, it is important to do some of this thinking in community, because other people can help us recognize and deal with unnamed presuppositions and gaps in logic.

We note three main patterns by which Christians often make this move. We use the illustration of moving from what biblical writers believed about hell to what we might believe as an example of how Christians might approach other historical and contemporary voices.

1. Some Christians take the Bible in a literal way—that is, assuming a one-to-one correlation between what the Bible asked readers in antiquity to believe and what we should believe today. For example, if a biblical witness depicts God casting the unfaithful into an "outer darkness, where there will be weeping and gnashing of teeth" (Matt 25:30), this group of interpreters will believe that such a fate awaits the unfaithful. When asked how to square this action with the notion that God acts in love, these interpreters reply that all deserve condemnation; however, as an act of grace, God in love offers the way to salvation. God will welcome into the world of salvation those who accept God's invitation to salvation and then live faithfully. Those who reject the offer and live unfaithfully receive the condemnation they deserve.
2. Many Christians recognize differences in the ancient and contemporary views of the universe and want to take account of other cultural differences between the past and the present, to "translate" ancient views of hell into contemporary equivalents. These Christians do not take hell to be a literal place of fire but identify other modes of suffering that God assigns because of disobedience. These folk are aware that they are not simply repeating the biblical way of thinking but are adapting it in light of a contemporary understanding of the universe. To return to an earlier example, some folk may think that hell is the painful sense of being alienated from God in the present and continuing beyond death, perhaps in magnified form. This viewpoint also faces the theological question of how to make sense of saying that God acts out of love when God condemns people to an eternity of alienation.
3. Some Christians believe they have the freedom to disagree with the Bible and with many voices in Christian tradition. When it comes to hell, these people insist that God's love overrides all other divine behaviors and that a loving God could not sentence people to suffering, even in the reduced terms of painful alienation from God. God's fundamental purpose is to redeem all.

This point of view faces the question of accountability. Do those who have been unfaithful get off scot-free? If so, is that fair or just to those who have been faithful, and especially to those whose faithfulness has caused them to suffer in this present life?

While we think that these three patterns of moving from biblical portrayals of hell as a place in the afterlife to contemporary beliefs about hell are workable, we need to remember that the lines between these patterns are sometimes arbitrary. Moreover, these may not be the only ways that people sort through what they believe about hell.

The Plan of This Book

This book is divided into four parts that move chronologically from the time of the Bible into the present.

Part 1 considers voices on hell in the world of the Bible. We begin (chap. 1) with a study of present and future punishment in the Old Testament. Significant developments in the move toward a notion of hell took place in Jewish literature from 300 BCE to 200 CE (chap. 2). The heart of part 1 is chapter 3, which focuses on how the concept of hell functions in the New Testament, taking into account apocalyptically oriented books—Mark, Matthew, the Lukan literature, Paul's letters, several other letters, and of course the book of Revelation—as well as the Gospel and Letters of John.

Part 2 focuses on voices on hell from the early history of the church up to the twentieth century. We cover many centuries and listen to many voices from many places. In chapter 4 we go from the second century CE to the Reformation (early sixteenth century) and consider such material as the Apocalypse of Paul, Cyprian of Carthage, Origen, and Augustine. This chapter traces the emergence of the doctrine of purgatory.

Chapter 5 takes in the Protestants Luther and Calvin and the Catholic Ignatius Loyola, among others. John Wesley deserves mention, as does Jonathan Edwards and his famous sermon "Sinners in the Hands of an Angry God." Part 2 wraps up with a look at how hell was discussed in popular religious life in the late nineteenth and early twentieth centuries.

Part 3 brings the discussion into the contemporary era with voices that nuance their views of hell or move away from the traditional views. These viewpoints include Roman Catholic perspectives (chap. 6). Some voices modernize the view of hell through a process called demythologizing (chap. 7). Others take the language of hell in more figurative or metaphorical directions, following the lead of Karl Barth, Emil Brunner, and theologians within the postliberal movement (chap. 8). Jürgen Moltmann and others offer the possibility of escaping from hell (chap. 9). A more complicated discussion takes place in connection with liberation theology as well as the idea that some people believe that sin in the present brings about punishment in the present (through social process) with little consideration of what might happen in the afterlife (chap. 10). Those who follow open and relational theologies tend to believe that hell does not exist as a fiery place of punishment. Marjorie Suchocki and some other process theologians envision hell as a function of consciousness and offer a range of possibilities from choices in the afterlife through universal salvation to the idea that at death, consciousness simply stops. There is no hell because there is no awareness after death (chap. 11).

Part 4 is a summary of the three main views that weave in and out of the periods of the Bible and the history of the church: hell as a place of eternal punishment (chap. 12); annihilationism, sometimes called the conditional view of hell (chap. 13); and universalism, the view that there is no hell because all will be saved (chap. 14).

The book proper concludes with an afterword in which the authors straightforwardly say what we believe about hell. In the manner of sharing among friends, we explain what we believe and why. We hope that having these two statements and interchange between the authors illustrates one of the goals of the book in that we share our different accents of conviction in a context of respect for one another.

The book contains suggestions for further reading for those who wish to dive more deeply into the subject. The entries are lightly annotated.

This volume includes a study guide that can be used by small groups and individuals. The study is set up for five sessions, but the material can be telescoped into three sessions or expanded to more than five. The study guide, like the book itself, is designed to help bring options to the surface and to provide prompts for conversation that help participants listen to and identify possible views of hell that make the most sense to the reader. The study guide will help readers reflect on the consequences of how congregations live and witness and will help readers compare and contrast those consequences so they will be in positions to make conscientious choices that are appropriate to their deepest beliefs.

Online Resource for Preaching

Although we wrote this book with a general audience in mind, we hope preachers will find the material of interest, so we developed an online resource to help preachers engage the notion of hell in the pulpit. The resource includes a general orientation to the subject and suggestions for sermon series based on biblical texts and topics. It deals with preaching in conversation with hell in the Christian year and the Revised Common Lectionary, in free selection of texts. We raise the possibility of preaching topical sermons on hell and discuss possible sermon series. This resource is available free of charge at www.wjkbooks.com/Hell.

Sending This Book Forward in Hope

As we point out in a section above, "Why Devote a Book to the Topic of Hell?," this work is being published in a chaotic and treacherous season of history. We hope and pray it can help readers strengthen their resolve to live according to God's intentions for the communities of humankind and nature to live together in love, peace, justice, freedom, and abundance. Put negatively, for those who believe in hell, this book might be a pastoral warning to avoid contributing to the violation of God's purposes that bring about suffering in the present and that could lead to their own eternal punishment. For those who do not believe in hell, the book might function as a warning that while God does not directly consign us to punishment, attitudes and behavior that undermine God's intentions and abundance set in motion forces that can effectively turn a part of the world into a hell for us and unmitigated suffering for others. Put positively for those who believe in hell, this book is an invitation to live faithfully in ways that are consistent with God's purposes and that limit the possibilities of a final condemnation. Put positively for those who do not believe in hell, this volume might function similarly—as an invitation to cooperate with God and God's purposes in thinking and acting in ways that urge humankind and nature toward a world that promotes love, justice, peace, and abundance.

Part 1

Voices on Hell from the World of the Bible

In part 1 we look at how the concept of hell functions in the Bible. Chapter 1 sets the stage for the discussion by considering the role of punishment in the life of Israel. In chapter 2, we follow the emergence of the notion of hell in Jewish literature beginning about 300 BCE; chapter 3 sketches attitudes toward hell in the Gospels and Letters.

Chapter 1

Voices from the Old Testament

If this chapter were titled "Hell in the Old Testament," it could be one of the shortest chapters in the history of publication, because the idea of hell as conscious ongoing punishment in the afterlife does not directly appear in the First Testament. However, two aspects of the Old Testament offer useful background on the concept of hell: (1) the notion of an afterlife called Sheol; (2) the broader notion of why God punishes Israel and others in the context of this life.

Sheol: The Afterlife in a Shadowy Underworld

The King James Version of the Bible often uses "hell" to translate the Hebrew word *sheol*. Psalm 139:8 is an example: "If I ascend up into heaven, thou art there: if I make my bed in hell, behold, thou art there." A person reading the psalm in English today could easily interpret "hell" in this context as a place of punishment and ask, "Why is the psalmist making a bed in such a place, and why is God there?" However, few English versions today translate *sheol* as "hell." Many versions simply render the Hebrew letters into English and speak directly of Sheol. Thus, we read, "If I make my bed in Sheol, you are there."

The word *sheol* refers to an afterlife, but not to a place of fiery punishment. To the Hebrews Sheol was a shadowy underworld where a form of a person goes at death. The Old Testament sometimes refers to the inhabitants of Sheol as "shades," suggesting

19

that they are shadows of their former selves (e.g., Job 26:5; Ps 88:10; Isa 14:9).

Some passages indicate that Sheol is a dark place (e.g., Job 17:13; Lam 3:6). Jacob goes down to Sheol in mourning because he grieves for Joseph, whom he presumes is dead (Gen 37:35). According to some writers, the dead do not praise God in Sheol (Ps 6:5; Isa 38:18). Sheol can represent the place of farthest removal from God (Ps 139:7–8; Amos 9:2). For Ecclesiastes, "there is no work or thought or knowledge or wisdom in Sheol" (Eccl 9:10). Some writers personify Sheol, that is, speak as if it is animated. For instance, Sheol is hungry to receive the living (Isa 5:14; Hab 2:5).

Sheol appears to be the destination of both the faithful (as in Gen 37:35; Job 21:13) and the unfaithful (e.g., Num 16:30; Pss 9:17; 31:17; 55:15; Isa 5:14; 14:11). Occasional passages cast a negative pall on Sheol (e.g., Pss 49:14; 116:3), but there is no extended suggestion that God actively rewards the faithful or actively punishes the unfaithful in Sheol.

The Septuagint, the translation of the Hebrew Bible into Greek, renders the Hebrew *sheol* into Greek with the word *hadēs*, which comes into English as "Hades." The translators of the Septuagint probably chose "Hades" because some of the Greeks used Hades as the name of the gatekeeper of the underworld. The underworld itself, accessed through gates, was sometimes called by the same name. This usage appears in the New Testament (e.g., Luke 16:23; Acts 2:27), as we note in chapter 3. The Old Testament itself, then, does not have a developed view of punishment in the afterlife. However, the idea of hell as a place of prolonged punishment does emerge in Jewish literature beginning about 300 BCE.

God Punishes People in This Life

We focus now on God directly punishing individuals, communities, and nations. The Old Testament contains far-reaching discussions of human crimes and punishment, including principles and mechanisms by which human agents pass judgment and inflict punishment. While that is an important topic, our focus in this section is on God's role as a direct punishing force.

Many biblical writers share the idea that things happen in the world either by God's immediate direction or with God's permission. According to this way of thinking, God sometimes directly orchestrates acts of punishment, but in other instances, human attitudes and behavior bring about circumstances that function as punishment. God does not directly push the button to start a punishment. However, God does not push the button to stop it, though God could. Either way—by direct initiation or passive permission—God is responsible for all that happens.

As we have previously made clear, the Old Testament does not envision significant punishment taking place in an afterlife. Instead, punishment takes place in the context of present life and history.

God punishes when human beings violate God's aims for the human family and for the created world. "Justice" (Heb. *mishpat*) is one of several biblical ways of speaking about what God hopes for the human family in relationship with other human beings, with animals, and with all other elements of nature. God seeks a world of justice, and God acts according to justice. Isaiah represents this dominant biblical view by declaring, "The LORD is a God of justice" (Isa 30:18). Justice is often paired with righteousness (Heb. *tsedeq*) as, for example, in Psalm 33:5, God "loves righteousness and justice." Righteousness is doing the "just thing," which, in the Bible, is to encourage people and nature to live together rightly, that is, in mutual support. Indeed, these two realities are the foundation of God's throne (Ps 97:2).

In the broad sense, justice has a relational meaning that refers to creating conditions whereby people and nature relate to one another in a mutually supportive community. People are righteous—they live rightly—when they live into the things that make for a just world. Genesis 1 depicts the fully just world as one in which each element of creation is honored in its own integrity and in which all things work together to create a world of blessing for each and all. To be righteous is to do what is right to encourage such a community. God, the paradigm of righteousness, always does what is right by inviting, creating, and maintaining a mutually supportive community in the pattern of Genesis 1. Theologian Clark M. Williamson writes that blessing is "*shalom* (peace) with oneself and, because we are related to all else that is, with God, and with all our neighbors, with all the living things in the environment that are also to be fruitful and multiply."[1]

God positively encourages the human community toward the possibility of living in justice. For example, through the mouth of Moses the writers of Deuteronomy admonish the covenantal community: "Justice, and only justice, you shall pursue" (Deut 16:20). For the writers of Deuteronomy, as for many others, the driving human purpose in covenantal living is to create a community in which all relationships are just, that is, in which everyone and everything has access to the things that make for support, in which everything works together for blessing for all.

There is a background notion here. God created the world out of the deep primeval chaos to be a network of interlocking and supportive relationships (Gen 1:1–2). But it was "a world in precarious balance, where every action (human or divine) affected the equilibrium toward either greater harmony or to chaos and destruction." God seeks to "maintain a balance in the universe that induces harmony and well-being." The practice of justice contributed to the stability of the world and its capacity to be fruitful and multiply. By contrast, "when someone violated individual or communal norms, that person [or group] tipped the balance away from shalom, threatening the community's prosperity and well-being." According to this ancient viewpoint, punishment can remove a threat to the just community and restore the balance of the universe.[2]

All talk about punishment in Israel takes place under the umbrella of God's overarching purpose to create a truly just world. To the best of our knowledge, the biblical writers never regard punishment as an end in itself. God never punishes in a mode of uncontrolled emotional outrage, as parents today sometimes do when confronted by defiant children. In a sentence, God uses punishment to remove threats to the community so that justice, righteousness, blessing, and all things that make for authentic community can prosper. While punishment may inflict immediate pain on specific individuals, communities, or nations, the eventual aim of punishment is the restoration of the circumstances that make for blessing. When God destroys (or allows destruction of) a community, one aim is to remove the threat posed by that community to the possibilities of blessing to others and to those within the community under punishment. Another aim is to awaken those in the community being punished to the fact of their disobedience. The biblical writers who tell of such things also do so to show the later readers what went wrong, why, and the consequences, so the readers will be forewarned and can avoid making their own versions of the same mistake(s).

It is helpful to distinguish the roles and emphases of punishment for Israel and for nations outside Israel. Within the covenantal community, Israel, punishment plays an instructional role. When people violate the things that make for justice, God seeks to prompt the community to return to just ways. God typically sends prophets and others to call the community to repent or face significant punishment (e.g., Hos 14:1–3). If people continue in disobedience, God punishes them with an eye toward repentance and restoration. In the version of the covenant in Deuteronomy 27–28, for example, when the people are obedient, blessing follows, but when they are disobedient God visits curses upon them. Malachi uses the language of purification by fire to speak of the role of punishment in the covenant. God "will sit as a refiner and purifier of silver, and [God] will purify the descendants of Levi and refine them like gold and silver" (Mal 3:3). If it is too late for those in view to repent and turn toward obedience, then the later readers can be forewarned and learn from the disobedience of those who came before.

Beyond the covenantal community, God sometimes punishes peoples and nations who engage in injustice against Israel, who lead Israel into living unjustly, or who otherwise violate God's purposes of blessing for all (e.g., Isa 21:1–10). God's capacity to punish other nations (e.g., causing them to fall) demonstrates the power of God over other gods in the plain sight of both the nations and Israel. This awareness strengthens Israel to remain faithful to God even when confronted by challenges from other peoples. It also reveals the strength of God's commitment to creating circumstances that are ripe for blessing by removing the menace to those circumstances posed by other peoples.

At one time there were no limits on human retribution in the ancient Near East. If one villager kidnapped a member of another village, the second group could destroy the first village. But the

Code of Hammurabi (roughly 1750 BCE) enshrines the idea—accepted later in Israel—that punishment should be meted out in proportion to the violation (and not in excess), "an eye for an eye" (Exod 21:23–27). The extent of the punishment points to the extent of the violation.

It is important to note that the biblical writers imply a similar reciprocity between human violation and divine punishment. God enacts judgment measure-for-measure in relationship to the degree of disobedience. Moreover, the prophets point to a "*correspondence* between sin and judgment, crime and punishment." The punishment is "according to, in some way like, or appropriate in either a literal or symbolic fashion, to the sin committed."[3] Thus Obadiah 15 says,

> As you have done, it shall be done to you;
> your deeds shall return on your own head.

Patrick Miller Jr. writes, "The judgment is not independent of the crime or sin. Rather it is rooted directly in the sin in a relationship of deed and its consequence. The evil that one does comes back upon the sinner even as the good comes upon the righteous." To put it another way, God "brings back not some strange 'punishment' as a result [of a violation] but something indissolubly linked to the deed."[4] Here, too, the nature and extent of the punishment point back to the nature and extent of the violation.

This principle is quite important when interpreting the nature and extent of the punishment meted out through hell. In that world, the punishment is itself an index of the significance of the violation. A severe punishment means that a severe violation has occurred. A violation that merits burning forever is a fundamental threat to the purposes of God.

In some cases, the effects of punishment continue for long periods of time. Indeed, in some cases life is changed significantly after the punishment. After Cain kills Abel, for example, Cain cannot take corrective action by realigning his values and behavior with God in relationship to his brother, because Abel is dead. But as an act of grace, God places a mark on Cain so that others would not kill him (Gen 4:15–17). God's behavior with Cain illustrates a pattern: when God visits a punishment that does not permit restoration of community, God often provides a measure of grace so that those who are punished can live as fully into God's purposes as their situation allows.

Occasionally, God punishes a people with complete destruction and death (e.g., Exod 14:26–29). God appears to take this action to end a significant threat to God's purposes posed by the people whom God destroys. This notion will recur when we discuss the transition from punishment in the present life to punishment in the afterlife by means of consigning people to hell. Consignment to hell means that the violators can no longer pose a threat to covenantal community.

As this chapter closes, we may say almost categorically that the reason the biblical writers emphasize punishment is *to impress upon the hearers or readers* the importance of living faithfully according to the vision of the just community to be a part of the realm and to avoid punishment. The apostle Paul offers an example of this approach when he recalls the story in Exodus of the people of Israel who worshiped the golden calf. Paul admonishes the Corinthians, "Do not become idolaters as some of them did, as it is written, 'The people sat down to eat and drink, and they rose up to play'" (1 Cor 10:7; cf. Exod 32:6). Paul wants the Corinthians to avoid idolatry in their situation some thirteen hundred years after the exodus. By doing so, the Corinthians can be part of the movement toward the new world that Paul believed God was bringing about. In this case, as in many others, hearing about the punishment in the past allows the congregation to reflect on its situation and to reinforce its commitment to faithfulness or to take corrective action (e.g., repentance) to avoid the fate of the punished people and to realign the community's life with the purposes of God.

Many of these ideas raise important theological questions about God's love, mercy, compassion, and forgiveness for those who are punished. As we noted at the outset of this section, we put these and other questions on hold until the afterword, when the important matter of what we most deeply believe about God and punishment takes center stage.

Chapter 2

Voices from Early Judaism

*J*ewish writers begin to speak of punishment in the afterlife around 300 BCE. These notions are the seedbeds of the pictures of hell in the New Testament. We say "pictures" (plural) because different documents put forward somewhat different emphases. As we say so often when it comes to the Bible and Jewish tradition, there are different viewpoints. In this chapter we first provide an orientation to the contexts and reasons some Jewish writers turned to the idea of hell and then look at some texts that specifically anticipate conscious suffering in the afterlife for evildoers.

When and Why Did Jewish Writers Turn to the Notion of Hell?

The historical settings of Jewish life play an important role in understanding why the notion of hell emerged in Jewish thinking. Jewish history in the biblical period was often tumultuous, with invasion from the outside, struggle for control within, forays into idolatry, and prophetic confrontation interspersed with periods of justice, peace, and prosperity. In 586 BCE, the Babylonian Empire captured Jerusalem, destroyed the First Temple, burned much of the city, and sent many Jewish leaders into exile in Babylon.

From that time forward the Jewish people largely lived under the rule of outside empires. Cyrus the Persian liberated the exiles from Babylon in 539 BCE and allowed many Jews to return to their homeland, but they did so as a colony of Persia. In 332 BCE Alexander the Great conquered Galilee, Samaria, and Judea, and sought to infuse the population with Greek culture. A series of outside nations ruled the Jewish community, including Greeks, Egyptians, and Syrians. The Maccabean revolt (168–165 BCE) established independence that lasted from 165 to 63 BCE, when the Romans captured Jerusalem and took full control of the land. The Romans inflicted heavy taxes and ruled by violence. From 66 to 73 CE the Romans waged a savage war on the Jewish people, which included sacking Jerusalem and destroying the Second Temple in the year 70.

Our interest here is not simply in chronology but in the fact that for half a millennium, the Jewish people lived under oppression from outsiders. One empire after another inflicted its ways on the Jewish communities. Consequently, three important themes pervade many Jewish writings in this period: (1) They lament the continuous oppression and suffering. (2) They look for God to set things right. (3) Because some in the Jewish community were in danger of compromising or even drifting away from Judaism in the face of repression, the writings sought to persuade readers to remain faithfully practicing Jews.

In their appeal to readers to remain faithful, several Jewish writers contended that God would demonstrate God's faithfulness and power, and would vindicate the faithful, by interrupting the present age of history and replacing the world with a new creation. This transformation would include a great judgment at which God would welcome the faithful into the new world, often called the realm (or kingdom) of God, and God would consign the unfaithful to punishment in hell. The new creation would be the epitome of the just community described in Genesis 1 (see chap. 1). After the apocalypse—the great interruption—it would go on forever with no possibility of a return to chaos.

From the perspective of these early Jewish writers, the righteousness of God was at stake. For these writers, for God to be righteous, God must set things right with those who have suffered unjustly, especially the faithful. God sets things right by creating a new world. Some Jewish writers of the period believed that at death, each person goes to a Sheol-like room, waiting for the great cosmic interruption (an apocalypse). Others believed the consciousness of the individual is extinguished at death and is resurrected for the final judgment, at which point God keeps God's promises to the faithful by releasing them into a revivified world like that described in Genesis 1.

A Little Orientation to the Authors of Hell

Several of the apocalyptic thinkers—who appear to be the originators of the notion of hell as a place of fire—write in the name of figures who lived much earlier, such as Enoch, Ezra, and Baruch. The actual writers adopt these older names to add to the authority of their writings. They frequently speak in visions loaded with word pictures, often reminiscent of the book of Revelation. These authors use vivid language to speak of hell. Even when such language has symbolic overtones, it points to a real time of suffering on the part of the condemned. While we usually think of the inhabitants of hell as human beings, these documents sometimes include fallen angels and other suprahuman beings or use allegorical representations of people.

Background on Hades and Gehenna

As in the discussion of hell in the Old Testament, we need to pause over two words that appear again in this line of Jewish literature. The interpreter needs to consider each occurrence of "Hades" in light of its specific meanings. Most often in this literature, Hades is a shady underworld habitation of the dead similar to what is found in the Septuagint, the Greek translation of the Old Testament (e.g., 2 Macc 6:23; 1 En. 102.5; 103.7; 2 Bar. 23.4; cf. Pss. Sol. 14.9–10; Jub. 7.29; 22.22).[1] We encounter this way of thinking in Revelation 20:14. When God's final intervention in history (the apocalypse) occurs, Hades will give up its dead for the final judgment (e.g., 1 En. 51.3; 4 Ezra 4.42; 7.32; 2 Bar. 42.8). Beyond this idea of Hades as a waiting room for the dead, we find a few suggestions that punishment begins for the unfaithful in Hades (e.g., Sir 21:9–10; 1 En. 51.3; 63.10; 103.7–8; 4 Ezra 4.42; 7:32; 2 Bar. 42.8; 50.2). This view is evident in Luke 16:19–31.

Another word that factors into the discussion is "Gehenna." This comes from a Hebrew word (*ge-hinnom*) that means "Valley of Hinnom" and refers to a geographical location, a valley, just south of Jerusalem. The word comes through Greek and Latin into English as "Gehenna." According to a popular explanation, the Valley of Hinnom, Gehenna, was a garbage dump. This led some interpreters to think that the flames and smoke from the burning garbage gave rise to the idea of Gehenna (hell) as a place of fire and punishment. Some interpreters took this reference metaphorically and others literally. However, there is no evidence that people in antiquity thought of that valley as a garbage dump.

More likely, the ancients thought of the Valley of Hinnom in connection with punishment because idolatry took place there, including horrific child sacrifices to the god Molech (e.g., 2 Kgs 16:3; 21:6, 23). Moreover, the Babylonians slaughtered many Judeans there (Jer 7:29–34; 19:1–15). By the time of 1 Enoch (see below), some people regarded Gehenna as the name of the place where the final judgment would occur and punishment would begin (1 En. 26–27; 54.1–6; 56.1–4; Sib. Or. 1.100–103; 2.883–3.12).

Some Passages That Picture Hell

We look now at early snapshots of hell in Jewish literature. Many of these pictures use the language of fire. While we think the writers often had literal fire in mind, it is also important to remember that it is sometimes hard to know when a reference is literal or figurative. Moreover, this literature is diverse in the ways in which it describes what happens to the wicked after death. In addition to everlasting fire, some passages seem to refer to fire that burns sinners for limited periods of time as well as extended punishment that does not involve fire and punishment that ends with the condemned community losing awareness altogether.

A common thread in all Jewish references to punishment in the afterlife, whether ongoing or of limited duration, whether by fire or some other means, is to present the listener with suffering that is almost unimaginable so the listening community will want to take actions to avoid those fates. If the degree of punishment reveals the degree of the crime (see chap. 1), such language reveals the writers' perceptions of the degree of violence done to the world by those who are sent to hell.

The earliest developed picture of hell in Jewish writings occurs in 1 Enoch, some parts of which probably date to 300 BCE. In 1 Enoch 1–5, Enoch announces that God will bless the faithful and destroy the unfaithful. After this, the good angel Raphael takes Enoch on a tour of the future world and a vision of the human family being separated into groups after death because of the judgment of all. Sinners are being condemned on a day of judgment when they are separated from the faithful. Raphael explains what is happening:

> These three [compartments] have been made in order that the spirits of the dead might be separated. And in the manner in which the souls of the dead are separated (by) this spring of water with light upon it, in like manner, the sinners are set apart when they die and are buried in the earth and judgment has not been executed upon them in their lifetime, upon this great pain, until the great day of judgment—and to those who curse *(there will be) pain and plague forever, and the retribution of their spirits.* (1 En. 22.9–11; our italics)

The righteous rise to be with God on the great day of judgment, but the wicked suffer "forever." It is important to recognize that Enoch is not just concerned with sin at the level of attitudes within the self or personal moral behavior in interpersonal interactions. Enoch calls out violations with social effects that diminish the quality of life: The judge "will remove the kings and the mighty ones from their comfortable seats and the strong ones from their thrones. . . . The faces of the strong will be slapped and be filled with shame and gloom" (1 En. 46.4–6). The empires that seem so powerful in this world will be dismantled and their leaders consigned to punishment.

Another tradition in 1 Enoch describes future punishment as a season of fire. This association of fire with hell is likely inspired by some of the later books of the Hebrew Bible. This association occurs in Isaiah 66:24 but is also resonant in Deuteronomy 32:22; Isaiah 33:11–12; Ezekiel 38:22; Daniel 7:11; Joel 2:3; and Zephaniah 1:18. It seems clear here that punishment involves actual fire.

Some interpreters see a twist on the notion of judgment by fire in another passage in 1 Enoch, in which punishment by fire is temporary and followed by complete destruction of the condemned:

> All that which is (common) with the heathen shall be surrendered; the towers shall be inflamed with fire, and be removed from the whole earth. They shall be thrown into the judgment of fire, and perish in wrath and in the force of the eternal judgment. (1 En. 91.9)

The fire here appears to be painful but temporary: "They shall be thrown into the judgment of fire, and perish in wrath." The burning appears to have a stopping point for those who are punished, because they go out of existence. Later commentators refer to this phenomenon as annihilation. The self of the evildoer does not continue to suffer but is annihilated, while the righteous continue to live in the realm of God. As we noted in discussion of 1 Enoch 22.9–11, some other Jewish traditions in this period (including some writings in the New Testament) envision punishment in hell continuing forever.

The earliest idea of a developed afterlife beyond Sheol that appears in the Old Testament is in Daniel 12:2, from about 168–165 BCE. While Daniel does not give details, it points to suffering beyond the final judgment: "Many of those who sleep in the dust of the earth shall awake, some to everlasting life and some to shame and everlasting contempt."

A document known as both 4 Ezra and 2 Esdras was likely put together relatively soon after the fall of the temple (70 CE). This passage brings together God's final intervention in history and what will happen to the faithful and unfaithful afterward:

> And the Most High shall be revealed upon the seat of judgment, and compassion shall pass away, and patience shall be

> withdrawn, but judgment alone shall remain, truth shall stand, and faithfulness shall grow strong. And recompense shall follow, and the reward shall be manifested; righteous deeds shall awake, and unrighteous deeds shall not sleep. Then the pit of torment shall appear, and opposite it shall be the place of rest; and the furnace of Hell [Gehenna] shall be disclosed, and opposite it the Paradise of delight. (4 Ezra 7.33–37)

This passage, like 1 Enoch, imagines hell as a place of fire. The Greek word behind "the furnace of fire" in this English translation of 4 Ezra 7.36 is *gehenna*.

A document titled 2 Baruch (late first century or early second century CE) develops a similar picture of suffering in the afterlife. In this excerpt, we see not only the nature of hell but also how the writer hopes the listeners will respond: because of receiving this vision, Baruch pleads with the recipients to repent and avoid the horrors that the document depicts. Baruch describes the future:

> For behold, the Most High will cause all these things to come [for judgment]. There will not be an opportunity to repent anymore, nor a limit to the times, nor a duration of the periods, nor a chance to rest, nor an opportunity to prayer, nor sending up petition, nor giving knowledge, nor giving love, nor opportunity of repentance, nor supplicating for offenses, nor prayers of the [parents], nor intercession of the prophets, nor help of the righteous. There is the proclamation of judgment to corruption, regarding the way to the fire and the path that leads to the glowing coals. (2 Bar. 85.10–13)

This continues a line of thought similar to 1 Enoch and 4 Ezra.

The idea of long-lasting punishment by fire in a world beyond the present one is not limited to apocalyptic literature. A philosophical tract called 4 Maccabees, written about the first century CE, refers to such fire. The book foresees punishment for a tyrant who has persecuted the Jews: "Justice will hold you in store for a fiercer and an everlasting fire and for torments which will never let you go for all time" (4 Macc 12:12; cf. 9:9). The book of Judith, written in roughly 100 BCE, affirms that God will punish the nations that rise up against Israel by sending "fire and worms into their flesh; they shall weep in pain forever" (Jdt 16:17). According to book 4 of the Sibylline Oracles, probably written shortly after the New Testament, God will judge "the impious" and send them "down into the gloom in fire" (Sib. Or. 4.43). The Testament of Judah, also likely penned after the New Testament, anticipates the time when "there shall no more be Beliar's spirit of error, because he will be thrown into eternal fire" (T. Jud. 25.3).

To look ahead for a moment: In our view, this is the basic perception of hell that we encounter in the New Testament.

Purposes of Hell

In this scenario, the main purposes of punishment that we identified in chapter 1 help us understand the purposes of hell. Perhaps the most important purpose is that by consigning the disobedient to hell, God assures the faithful that threats to blessing are permanently removed from the community. God's vision for justice, righteousness, and peace can unfold without interruption. The community of the new age is thus free to live fully and unhesitatingly in the realm of God. Moreover, the disobedient experience the consequences of their disobedience. They experience the qualities of existence in the afterlife that they brought about in the community during their lifetimes.

Some readers may object, "But the punishment that comes from being in hell is so much more painful than the disruptions the people under punishment caused while they were alive. The punishment seems disproportionate to the crime. It does not seem fair." Here the conception of correspondence between the sin and the punishment that we discussed in chapter 1 comes into play. From the perspective of the Jewish writers, the nature and extent of the punishment reveals the nature and extent of the crime. The fact that the wicked are consigned to fire reveals the writers' interpretations of the degree to which the wicked damaged the community and the degree to which they displeased God. The intensity of the fire exposes the seriousness of the crime. Things such as idolatry, falsehood, injustice, exploitation, slavery, and rule by violence have the effect of destroying the community by fire.

We emphasize that the notion of hell was developed as part of the response to the empires that despoiled Jewish life. Christians often think the idea of hell pertains only to individuals in the afterlife. While that dimension is not missing in Jewish antiquity, it is incomplete. The old age–new age dynamic that is central to apocalyptic literature is a direct criticism of the idolatrous, self-serving, people-exploiting empires that ruled the Jews. The empires themselves are condemned at the final judgment, and their leaders and structures are cast into the fiery pit, never to rise again.

Many writers in the world of biblical antiquity use the possibility of suffering in hell to motivate listeners to repent. The descriptions of hell are a part of the reason to turn away from complicity with the old age—with its idolatry, falsehood, and violence—and to turn toward the realm of God. From this point of view, visions of hell are pastoral warnings. They are intended to motivate people to turn toward the realm and eternal safety. This purpose underlies the function of hell in the New Testament.

Chapter 3

Voices from the New Testament

*O*n the one hand, nearly every document in the last twenty-seven books of the Bible refers to punishment in the afterlife; some documents even anticipate punishment beginning in this life. Punishment is typically described in one of two ways—as continued, ongoing suffering (as in continuously burning flames of fire) or as a singular act of punishment (annihilation or destruction). It is not always possible to determine the precise nature of the punishment particular biblical writers had in mind. As in so many things related to the Bible, the clusters of viewpoints are diverse.

When it comes to direct references to hell or destruction, there are fewer than many Christians expect to find. Furthermore, New Testament references, while often gruesome, are typically not as vivid as pictures of hell or destruction in Jewish literature from the same period.

Many New Testament writers did not need to delineate details about hell because many of their listeners *assumed* pictures of punishment beyond death like those described in chapter 2. They could bring hell to the mind of the listener with key words and phrases. At the same time, we should not speak of *the* concept of hell in the New Testament but should try to identify the nuances of viewpoint from author to author.

The New Testament writers use the notion of hell in the same ways as their Jewish compatriots discussed in chapter 2. They mention hell to motivate the congregations to whom they wrote to turn away from collusion with the old age, especially with its idolatry, injustice, exploitation, violence, and other forms of cooperation with empire, and to continue on the faithful pathway to the final and full manifestation of the realm of God and avoid an afterlife of punishment. When viewed in this light, the New Testament references to hell have a pastoral purpose: they are intended to encourage listeners toward faithfulness.

We do not have space to discuss every allusion to hell in the New Testament, but we can look at representative passages. In this chapter, we first consider references to hell in Mark, Matthew, and Luke-Acts. We turn then to Paul and the later letters. The book of Revelation deserves a stop before taking up the Gospel and Letters of John, as well as the book of Hebrews.

People who lived in the period of the New Testament, like their Jewish ancestors, often spoke in images, metaphors, and symbols. It is sometimes difficult to determine whether a writer intends a statement about hell to be taken literally or symbolically. This is especially true of references to hell as a place of fire. The Jewish sources reported in chapter 2 seem to regard hell as a place of fiery punishment, so it is reasonable to think that the New Testament writers often had a similar viewpoint. However, we recognize that some passages are ambiguous in this regard, and occasional passages seem to be symbolic.

Hell in Mark, Matthew, and Luke-Acts

Mark, Matthew, and Luke tell the story of Jesus in similar ways, although each author adapts that story for their particular congregations and settings. In addition, Luke wrote Acts to continue the story of Jesus as it was taken up by the church.

These Gospels and Acts are apocalyptic in that they present God beginning to effect the transition from the present old age to the realm of God. The distinctive note in the Gospels and Acts is that God is working through the ministry of Jesus, and later the church, to partially manifest the realm and will fully bring the realm at the second coming of Christ, when God will bring an end to the old world and fully manifest the new. Then will come God's final judgment, when those who have been faithful to the values and practices of the realm will be welcomed into it, while those who violated the values and practices will be condemned to hell. We find this apocalyptic thinking in the first three Gospels, Acts, the letters of Paul and others, and Revelation.

This end-time idea is explicit in the preaching of John the Baptist early in Matthew and Luke when John declares that the ax is already laid to the root of the tree and that the tree that does not bear good fruit will be thrown into the fire. Moreover, God will burn the chaff (the unfaithful) with "unquenchable fire"—that is, the fire of hell (Matt 3:7–12; Luke 3:7–9).

In the first three Gospels, Jesus announces the coming of the realm as the main theme in his ministry (Mark 1:14–15; Matt 4:12–17; Luke 4:14–30). Although these passages do not directly mention hell, these texts are cases in which listeners would hear the announcement, especially the call to repent, implying the possibility of condemnation and punishment.

Mark. While the Gospel of Mark gives the least explicit attention to hell among the first three Gospels and Acts, the main motif in Mark—the partial manifestation of the realm in the present through the ministry of Jesus and its final manifestation at the second coming—presumes the possibility of hell. The reference to eternal punishment using "Gehenna" to evoke the notion of hell appears three times in the forceful passage Mark 9:42–48:

> If any of you cause one of these little ones who believe in me to sin, it would be better for you if a great millstone were hung around your neck and you were thrown into the sea. If your hand causes you to sin, cut it off; it is better for you to enter life maimed than to have two hands and to go to hell [*gehenna*], to the unquenchable fire. And if your foot causes you to sin, cut it off; it is better for you to enter life lame than to have two feet and to be thrown into hell [*gehenna*]. And if your eye causes you to sin, tear it out; it is better for you to enter the [realm] of God with one eye than to have two eyes and to be thrown into hell [*gehenna*], where their worm never dies and the fire is never quenched.

To sin, for Mark, is to turn off the pathway to the realm or to encourage others to do so.

The Jewish community did not practice self-mutilation as part of its religious life. But as we have seen, many people in that world did believe in a fiery punishment. It seems unlikely that Mark wanted people literally to cut off hands and feet, but the writer uses this language to stress the importance of taking dramatic action (repentance) to avoid being cast into hell, "where their worm never dies and the fire is never quenched."

Matthew. The Gospel of Matthew gives considerably more attention than Mark to the possibility of hell. Matthew's references to hell generally serve to encourage members of the Matthean congregation to live as faithful disciples in the ways of the realm that Jesus teaches, therefore avoiding hell. In the Sermon on the Mount, the Matthean Jesus indicates that those who disrupt relationships in the church—the community that is supposed to embody the realm—by calling others "fool" will be "liable to the hell [*gehenna*] of fire" (Matt 5:22). Matthew follows Mark in advising his disciples to tear out an eye and cut off a hand to remove the agencies to sin rather "than for your whole body to be thrown into hell [*gehenna*]" (5:29–30). When counseling the disciples to prepare for persecution as they follow his way, the Jesus of the First Gospel declares, "Do not fear those who kill the body but cannot kill the soul; rather, fear the one who can destroy both soul and body in hell [*gehenna*]" (Matt 10:28).

Matthew ends the parable of Separation of the Weeds and the Wheat with a stern warning: "Collect the weeds first and bind them in bundles to be burned, but gather the wheat into my barn" (Matt 13:30). Interpreting the allegorical significance of that parable, the Matthean Jesus says the field hands will gather "all causes of sin and all evildoers" and will "throw them into the furnace of fire, where there will be weeping and gnashing of teeth" (13:41–42). Making a similar point later in the Gospel, Jesus slightly intensifies the picture of hell: "It is better for you to enter life with one eye than to have two eyes and to be thrown into the hell [*gehenna*] of fire" (18:9).

In a prophetic condemnation, Jesus claims that the Pharisees make a new convert "twice as much a child of hell [*gehenna*] as yourselves" (Matt 23:15). Indeed, Jesus says to the Pharisees, "You brood of vipers! How can you escape the judgment of hell [*gehenna*]?" (23:33).

Matthew offers one of the most existentially gripping biblical presentations of hell outside the book of Revelation in the four parables in Matthew 24:45–25:46. The first story recounts a wicked slave left in charge of a house who abuses the other slaves, only to hear this verdict when the owner returns: The owner will cut that slave into "pieces and put him with the hypocrites, where there will be weeping and gnashing of teeth" (24:51). While not including a direct reference to hell, the parable of the Ten Bridesmaids says the bridegroom arrives and takes the five wise bridesmaids into the house, "and the door was shut" (25:10). The five foolish bridesmaids are denied entrance into the wedding, that is, they are denied a place in the realm (25:11–12). In the parable of the Talents, the landowner gives five, two, and one talent, respectively, to three slaves with the instruction to multiply them, that is, to expand their witness to the realm. The slaves with five and two talents double their number. The landowner responds in acid terms to the servant who buried the one talent, "As for this worthless slave, throw him into the outer darkness, where there will be weeping and gnashing of teeth" (25:30). The parable of the Sheep and Goats envisions the final judgment, with the sheep, the righteous, being welcomed into "eternal life," the final and full manifestation of the realm, but the goats, the unfaithful, hearing the brutal sentence, "You who are accursed, depart from me into the eternal fire prepared for the devil and [the devil's] angels" (25:41).

The latter is an "eternal punishment" (Matt 25:41, 46). Occasionally Christians argue that "eternal punishment" refers to an "age" with a starting point and an ending point. However, "eternal" (Gk. *aiōnios*) typically means time going on without end (e.g., Ps 125:1; Isa 40:8; Ezek 27:36; 1 En. 102.3; cf. Matt 19:29).

Matthew twice refers to Hades. Jesus pronounces woes (judgment) on unrepentant cities, saying that Capernaum, one such city, will be "brought down to Hades" (Matt 11:20–24). Jesus declares that "the gates of Hades will not prevail against" the church (16:13–20). While we noted in chapters 1 and 2 that the word "Hades" could speak simply of the abode of the dead, the Matthean context suggests that Matthew has something more in mind. On the great day of judgment, those in Matthew's generation who do not repent (such as the residents of Chorazin and Bethsaida) will find it more intolerable than it will be for Tyre and Sidon—cities that were synonymous with evil in an earlier day (11:20–22). Indeed, unrepentant Capernaum (a city with which Jesus was closely associated) "will be brought down to Hades." On that day of judgment, it will be "more tolerable for the land of Sodom" than for Capernaum (11:23–24). While the phrase "gates of Hades" could refer simply to the entrance to the underworld (e.g., Isa 38:10), Matthew's expression "prevail against" suggests conflict, as if the occupants of Hades had the power to threaten the church and its witness to the realm. Matthew assures the congregation that their adversaries, even those lodged in hell, cannot overwhelm the church's witness to the realm.

Luke and Acts. The Gospel of Luke and the book of Acts (like the Gospel of Mark) give relatively little explicit attention to the notion of hell, but as we can see from key passages, the prospect of hell is in the background for those who do not recognize the apocalyptic work of God in Jesus. As in Mark and Matthew, Luke uses the preaching of John the Baptist to interpret the ministry of Jesus as one that invites listeners to repent of cooperating with Satan and the rulers of the old age and to join the movement toward the realm, or to face the consequences. According to John the Baptist, Jesus' "winnowing fork is in his hand to clear his threshing floor and to gather the wheat into his granary, but the chaff he will burn with unquenchable fire" (Luke 3:17; cf. 3:9).

The Lukan Jesus, like the Matthean Jesus, exhorts the disciples to persist in faithful witness even when the rulers of the old age seek to silence them: "Do not fear those who kill the body and after that can do nothing more. But I will show you whom to fear: fear the one who, after killing, has authority to cast into hell [*gehenna*]" (Luke 12:4–5). God will invite those who "enter through the narrow door" into the realm of God while saying to evildoers, "Go away from me" and sending them where "there will be weeping and gnashing of teeth" (13:24, 27–28). Anticipating God's final intervention in history, Jesus recalls fire and sulfur raining from heaven and destroying the wicked of Lot's day and says, "It will be like that on the day that the Son of Man is revealed" (17:29–30).

Concerning Hades, Luke follows Matthew in having Jesus compare the unrepentant people of Luke's own time with unrepentant people of Tyre and Sidon (Luke 10:13–14; cf. Ezek 26:1–27:36; 28:20–24) and Capernaum (Luke 10:15; cf. Isa 14:13–15). The Lukan Jesus implies that those who do not repent will face the same judgment as Tyre and Capernaum: being "brought down to Hades" (Luke 10:15). Regardless of the fact the Bible might elsewhere use "Hades" to refer to the nondescript underworld of the dead, Luke pictures Hades as a place of torment where one of the inhabitants (a wealthy person who did not repent of collaborating with the rulers of the old age) cries out, "I am in agony in these flames" (Luke 16:19–31, esp. vv. 22b–23).

In the two places the word "Hades" appears in the book of Acts, the author cites a quotation from the Old Testament in which Hades is the netherworld of the dead. Acts 2:25–28 cites Psalm 16:8–11. Acts 2:31 zeroes in on Psalm 16:10. In the Septuagint, Psalm 16:8–11 refers to Hades only as the abode of the dead. However, the explicit association of Hades with punishment in Luke 16:22b–23 suggests that Hades is a place of eternal discomfort in Acts 2:25–28 and 2:31. God did not abandon Jesus to punishment but, on the contrary, God exalted Jesus to God's right hand (Acts 2:25, 34; 7:56).

In the book of Acts, speakers often seek to persuade their audiences to repent and join the movement toward the realm by offering the positive aspects of salvation. For example, Peter calls the people to turn (repent) "so that your sins may be wiped out, so that times of refreshing may come" (Acts 3:19–20). While Acts does not use the word "hell" (*gehenna*) or directly dangle the threat of eternal fire before listeners, this volume still presumes the teaching on hell present in the Gospel of Luke. The great emphasis in Acts on the need for repentance to be saved presupposes salvation from punishment for sin (Acts 2:38; 8:22; cf. 20:21; 26:20). Peter promises that "everyone who calls on the name of the Lord shall be saved," implying that those who do not repent and call on the name of the Lord will not be saved (Acts 2:21). On the Areopagus, Paul declares flatly, "While God has overlooked the times of human ignorance, now [God] commands people everywhere to repent because [God] has fixed a day on which [God] will have the world judged in righteousness by [one] whom [God] has appointed" (Jesus) (Acts 17:30–31; cf. 10:42). Those who do not repent will be "rooted out of [God's] people," presumably in both this age and the age to come (Acts 3:23).

Final Punishment in the Letters of Paul

The apostle Paul was under the apocalyptic conviction that God is about to end the present evil age with a cosmic interruption (an apocalypse) by sending Jesus from heaven and replacing the present age with a new one (e.g., Rom 8:18–25; 1 Cor 1:7–8; 7:29–31; 11:26; esp. 15:1–57; 2 Cor 4:16–5:10; Phil 1:6, 3:20; 4:5; 1 Thess 2:19; 3:13; 4:13–18). This new world is called, among other things, the realm of God (Rom 14:17; 1 Cor 4:20; 6:9–10; 15:24, 50; Gal 5:21; 1 Thess 2:12).

This season of transition from the old to the new includes the final judgment when God would welcome into the new age those who worshiped and served the one true God but would consign the unfaithful to punishment. Amid a controversy in the church at Rome in which members were disrespecting one another, for example, Paul says, "Why do you pass judgment on your brother or sister? Or you, why do you despise your brother or sister? For we will all stand before the judgment seat of God.... Each one of us will be held accountable" (Rom 14:10, 12; our italics). Referring to the last day as the day of wrath, the apostle speaks bracingly to the congregation in Rome about gentiles in the community who have not fully converted to the living God but continue to follow some gentile beliefs and behaviors:

> Do you not realize that God's kindness is meant to lead you to repentance? But by your hard and impenitent heart you are storing up wrath for yourself on the day of wrath, when God's righteous judgment will be revealed. [God] will repay according to each one's deeds: to those who by patiently doing good seek for glory and honor and immortality, [God] will give eternal life, while for those who are self-seeking and who obey not the truth but injustice, there will be wrath and fury. There will be affliction and distress for everyone who does

evil, both the Jew first and the Greek, but glory and honor and peace for everyone who does good, both the Jew first and the Greek. For God shows no partiality. (Rom 2:4b–11; for similar sentiments: Rom 2:1–3; 3:5; 13:11–14; 14:10; 1 Cor 2:6; 5:5; 11:27–32; 2 Cor 5:10; Gal 5:16–21; 1 Thess 1:9–10; 3:13; 4:16–5:5; 5:23)

Paul does not employ the words *gehenna* or "Hades" in his letters. When referring to punishment, Paul often speaks of "the wrath [Gk. *orgē*] of God," as in the quote immediately above. Paul draws partly on the idea of the wrath of God in the Old Testament, where the phrase typically refers to God sending a catastrophe to punish Israel or the nations during present history (e.g., Isa 1:24; Jer 7:20; Ezek 7:8; Amos 1:11; Nah 1:6). However, interpreters often note that by the late Old Testament period, some of the prophets moved toward the idea of an apocalyptic destruction and transformation. Zephaniah is a paradigmatic example. The prophet imagines God speaking to a disobedient people (Judah): "I will utterly sweep away everything from the face of the earth. . . . That day will be a day of wrath, a day of distress and anguish, . . . of ruin and devastation. . . . The whole earth shall be consumed." It is "a terrible end" (Zeph 1:2, 15, 18). The prophet speaks similarly about God's judgment on Judah's enemies (2:1–15). Only when the devastation is complete will God restore Judah and the nations (3:8–20). Moving ahead to the time of Paul, several Jewish writers seem to promote the idea that the final condemnation is annihilation, that is, destruction (e.g., Pss. Sol. 15.4–5; Jub. 36.10; Sib. Or. 4.155–160; Sir 36:9–11).

As we observe in chapter 2, some Jewish writers in Paul's world associate the wrath of God with fire. For instance, a document added by Christians in the third century CE, 4 Ezra, asks, "Fire will go forth from [God's] wrath, and who is there to quench it?" (4 Ezra 16.9). This shows that some Christians were associating God's wrath with fire by that time. Paul, however, never speaks of the consequence of condemnation in the language of fire. Nor does Paul speak directly of continuing punishment in the afterlife. By contrast, the apostle does describe the path of the faithful into the postapocalyptic world of the realm, expounding on that life in detail in 1 Thessalonians 4:13–5:5 and 1 Corinthians 15. Our interpretive sense is that Paul foresees the destruction (annihilation) of the self as the consequence of disobedience.

However, any discussion of the wrath of God in Paul must also mention Paul's perception that the wrath of God was already in operation in a limited way. Bible students often speak of the "already . . . not yet" in relationship to the realm of God. Aspects of the realm are "already" appearing in the present, but the full manifestation of the realm is "yet to come" as it awaits the second coming of Jesus. Paul signals a similar understanding of the final condemnation by saying, "For the wrath of God is revealed from heaven against all ungodliness and injustice" (Rom 1:18). The verb "is revealed" is present tense. The meaning is "for the wrath of God is now being revealed." Wisdom of Solomon helps us understand *how* this wrath is taking place when it states "that one is punished by the very things by which one sins" (Wis 11:16).

According to this way of thinking, sin creates circumstances in life that deprive the sinner and the sinful community of fullness of life and blessing and leave people moving toward destruction. The broken circumstances of life are themselves a present punishment, with the final penalty (destruction) to come at God's climactic interruption of the present age; Paul adapts this perspective to the sin of idolatry in Romans 1:18–32. Worship of idols deceived people into thinking that the qualities of life identified with idolatrous communities are faithful when they actually destroy the self and community (e.g., Rom 1:26–32). God did not actively visit punishment on the community but "God gave them over" to their sin. This sin brings about the personal and social collapse that is itself the punishment.

Readers are likely to agree with Paul that things like injustice, covetousness, malice, and murder (among the behaviors mentioned in Rom 1:28–32) violate God's purposes. For Paul, when such things occur in life, they are simultaneously a violation and punishment in that they undermine the life of blessing that God intends. However, the interpretation of interaction between people of the same sex in Romans 1:26–28 is contested in the church today. We do not have space to enter into that discussion in this book. However, so readers will not be distracted by wondering what Bob and Ron think, we indicate that we share progressive theological views holding that a variety of relationships among people of the same and different sexualities can be God-given.[1] Regardless of how the reader interprets these matters, Paul's larger point here is provocative; namely, when we are disobedient, we invite punishment on ourselves, and that punishment takes the form of a broken life that denies the fullness of blessing—and that can invoke suffering.

Stanley Stowers, who taught New Testament at Yale University, makes an important observation about Paul's perspective:

> God will sometime in the future have a great day of judgment in which [God] will justly mete out reward and punishment to Israel and the other peoples collectively and will also judge individual lives within those collectives. This idea of a judgment day addresses the problem of how those who are wicked (for example, attack, kill, and oppress others . . .) can be allowed to flourish while the good often suffer and live unrewarded. Ancient Jewish writings tend to think of this in collective and concrete terms . . . : for example, Babylon and Rome attacked and ravaged Judea. Paul also thinks collectively and concretely in speaking of Jews and Greeks ([Rom] 1:16; 2:10). The collective and the individual do not exclude one another.[2]

Rome is judged an oppressive social system. Individuals within the congregation (and in the world beyond) are judged for the degree to which they are faithful or complicit with idolatry in violation of the covenant.

Final Punishment among the Followers of Paul

Many scholars today opine that six letters that bear Paul's name were written after Paul's time by his followers. While this may seem like forgery to people today, it was a common (and respected) practice in Paul's time. A disciple would write in the name of a master to extend the master's teaching into a new situation. The letters that fall into this category are Ephesians, Colossians, 1 and 2 Timothy, Titus, and 2 Thessalonians.

All of these documents assume the apocalyptic worldview, but the first five letters give little attention to the nature of final punishment. What few remarks they do make follow in the train of Paul's thought discussed in the previous section of this chapter.

Ephesians. According to Ephesians 2:3, the readers and listeners had been "children of wrath," except for the grace of God through Jesus Christ. Receiving that grace brought with it the responsibility of living according to its values and practices. The members of the congregation are to stop such behaviors as bitterness, anger, wrangling, slander, and malice because "the wrath of God comes on those who are disobedient" (4:31; 5:6).

One passage in Ephesians has been the subject of intense debate among interpreters:

> But each of us was given grace according to the measure of Christ's gift. Therefore it is said,
>
> > "When he ascended on high, he made captivity itself a captive; he gave gifts to his people."
>
> (When it says, "He ascended," what does it mean but that he had also descended into the lower parts of the earth? He who descended is the same one who ascended far above all the heavens, so that he might fill all things.) (4:7–10)

Scholars pose three main possibilities for interpreting the phrase in 4:9 that is key to our study, "He had also descended into the lower parts of the earth." (1) Many say it refers to the descent of Christ into hell. (2) Others take it to refer to the incarnation. Christ descended from heaven to become incarnate on the earth. (3) Still others take the expression to refer to Christ ascending to heaven and then sending down to the earth the Holy Spirit, through whom Christ gave gifts to the church that are so important in Ephesians 4:12–15.

We agree with the first position, but in a modified way. "Lower parts [Gk. *katōtera*] of the earth" almost certainly refers to the underworld (as do similar uses of "lower parts" [*katōtera*] in Pss 63:9; 86:13; 88:6; 139:15; Lam 3:55; Sir 51:6). However, the author shows no interest in the nature of the underworld either directly or by implication. Nor does the writer of Ephesians report what Christ did there. The clue to the reason the author includes this descent "into the lower parts of the earth" is in the larger purpose of Christ "to fill all things"—that is, Christ will bring all things under God's rule (Eph 4:10; cf. 1:8–10, 20–23). "All things" includes the "lower parts of the earth."

The affirmation in Ephesians that Christ has descended into the "lower parts of the earth" assures the community that even this dimension of life is under the sovereignty of God. The passage thus moves in the direction of the "harrowing of hell"—that is, the idea that Christ descended into the underworld to reclaim and redeem some (or all) who were there, a notion that is likely at least partially included in Christ filling all things. However, Ephesians 4:9 does not refer explicitly to some of the constituent elements usually associated with the harrowing of hell, such as Christ descending to hell between the crucifixion and resurrection.

Colossians, 1 and 2 Timothy, and Titus. The writer to the Colossians takes an approach to punishment in the afterlife similar to the writer of Ephesians without the reference to Christ descending into the lower parts of the earth. In Colossians, "the wrath of God is coming on those who are disobedient" because of "sexual immorality, impurity, passion, evil desire, and greed (which is idolatry)" (Col 3:5–6). To avoid the wrath of God, "now you must get rid of all such things" (3:8). Similarly, the Pastoral Letters—1 and 2 Timothy and Titus—presume the final judgment but they do not dwell on it, nor do they describe the punishment that results from disobedience (1 Tim 5:24; 2 Tim 4:1, 8).

2 Thessalonians. In contrast to Paul and the others who wrote in Paul's name, 2 Thessalonians gives graphic attention to the final judgment and its aftereffects. According to 2 Thessalonians, the community is suffering under persecution. But the righteous judgment of God will return Jesus and the "mighty angels" to the world "in a fiery flame, inflicting vengeance on those who do not know God and on those who do not obey the gospel of our Lord Jesus. These will suffer the punishment of eternal destruction, separated from the presence of the Lord and from the glory of his might" (1:8–9). This destruction (Gk. *olethros*) is "eternal" (*aiōnios*). By "eternal" the writer likely means ongoing, unceasing, or unending, the meaning in many other texts (e.g., Deut 15:17; Wis 10:14; 4 Macc 12:12; Matt 19:16; 25:46; 2 Cor 5:1). God will "repay with affliction those who afflict you" while providing relief for the afflicted (2 Thess 1:6–7).

The writer cautions the congregation not to follow a figure designated "the lawless one" (lawlessness is violating the divine purposes). The writer echoes Isaiah 11:4, which points to a day when God will destroy the wicked with "the breath of [God's] lips." Similarly, on the great day of revelation "the Lord Jesus will destroy with the breath of his [Jesus'] mouth, annihilating" the lawless one (2 Thess 2:8). "Destroy" (Gk. *anaireō*) means to bring to an end, to render powerless. The meaning of the word translated as "annihilating" (Gk. *katargeō)* is more complicated. At first sight, it seems to support that stream of interpreters who believe that hell is annihilation in the sense of the complete end of the self, including the loss of consciousness. To be sure, this verb often refers to death by warfare, murder, or execution (e.g., Gen 4:15; Wis 14:24; 4 Macc 18:11). However, as noted above, the writer of 2 Thessalonians likely foresees an eternal time of punishment. Indeed, the Psalms of Solomon, probably written a century or two before 2 Thessalonians, associates lawlessness with ongoing punishment: "The inheritance of sinners is destruction and darkness, and their lawless actions shall pursue them below into Hades" (Pss. Sol. 15.10).

Punishment in the Later Letters

The prospect of judgment followed by punishment appears prominently in the later letters of the New Testament. Here again, the writers seldom specify the particulars of punishment but assume that listeners will fill out the pictures based on commonly held perceptions. These writers urge listeners and readers to take corrective action to avoid punishment.

James. The theme of judgment and the potential of condemnation comes up repeatedly in the Letter of James (2:4, 13; 3:1; 4:12; 5:9). The writer exhorts the congregation to join faith with works and emphasizes the importance of loving the neighbor as the necessary correlate to faith. The writer is particularly concerned about the misuse of the tongue, which "sets on fire the cycle of life, and is itself set on fire by hell [*gehenna*]" (3:6). The presence of the word *gehenna* indicates that for James, the final condemnation is to the underworld of fire. No wonder James can say to the wealthy who exploit the poor, "Weep and wail for the miseries that are coming to you" (5:1).

1 Peter. The Letters of 1 and 2 Peter were probably written by followers in the tradition of Peter to invoke the apostle's authority for the documents. The persistent theme in 1 Peter is the call to the congregation to holy living, so they will be prepared to receive "an inheritance that is imperishable, undefiled, and unfading" (1:4; cf. 2:13–16). This call is urgent because the members of the community are suffering under persecution and in danger of drifting away. While the writer's appeal is largely positive, reminding the congregation of what they will inherit through holy living, the writer also warns that those "living in debauchery, passions, drunkenness, reveling, carousing, and lawless idolatry . . . will have to give an accounting to [the one] who stands ready to judge the living and the dead" (4:3, 5). The author asserts that the time is fast coming for the judgment.

However, revelers, drunks, and the lawless are not the only ones judged. To the surprise of many Christians, 1 Peter sees that judgment will "*begin* with the household of God; if it begins with us, what will be the end for those who do not obey the gospel of God?" (4:17; our italics).

The writer of 1 Peter asserts that after Christ had been raised from the dead, "he went and made a proclamation to the spirits in prison, who in former times did not obey, when God waited patiently in the days of Noah, during the building of the ark, in which a few, that is, eight lives, were saved" (3:19–20). Christians often cite this passage in support of the statement in the Apostles' Creed that "he descended into hell." The number of variations on the interpretations of this text are legion—where Christ went, when, and what he did there. These interpretations include the harrowing of hell. This is the idea, appealing to progressives, that Christ descended into hell to rescue some (or all) of the folk imprisoned there. Many people think Christ made this descent on Holy Saturday between the crucifixion and the resurrection.

However, an overwhelming number of biblical scholars today point to another interpretation.[3] They note that sources from the world of 1 Peter seldom refer to human beings as "spirits" and seldom refer to hell as a prison. The specific content of Jesus' message is not given. Instead, scholars note that the word "spirits" often refers to malevolent beings. According to Enoch, the "spirits" are angels who, before the flood, disobeyed God by having intercourse with human beings and bearing offspring. These offspring became a major source of evil in the world (1 En. 1–16, esp. 15.3–7; cf. Jub. 5.2–11; 10.1–14). Because of their disobedience, they were imprisoned, though the location of the prison is uncertain. The passage does not say that Jesus made this visit between the crucifixion and the resurrection. The Greek of the text does not say that Christ "descended" but uses a verb (*poreuomai*) that usually means "go" or "proceed" and is sometimes used to describe Christ's journey to the right hand of God (e.g., Acts 1:10–11). In this view, Christ stopped by the imprisoned spirits to demonstrate his final victory over them and over the consequences of their disobedience and to confirm their condemnation. God had waited in the days of Noah for them to repent, but they did not. As God saved the faithful in the time of Noah, so God would save the faithful at the last day. This affirmation was intended to encourage the congregation to remain faithful during their time of struggle as the proclamation confirmed the final victory of Christ.

In the past, Christians often regarded 1 Peter 4:6 as referring back to 3:19–20 when it says, "The gospel was proclaimed even to the dead." However, the reinterpretation of 3:19–20 calls for a reassessment of 4:6. The author reminds readers that they and their faith are regularly maligned by unbelieving gentiles (e.g., 3:16; 4:4). Many believers have died. The day is coming when they—and especially the unbelieving gentiles—will have to give an account to "the one who stands ready to judge the living and the dead" (4:5). The statement that "the gospel was proclaimed even to the dead" likely refers to the dead having heard the gospel while they were alive. The writer thus assures the living members of the congregation that those who preceded them in death will join them in the world to come.[4]

Jude and 2 Peter. It may seem strange to see Jude and 2 Peter discussed together. However, most scholars today think that Jude was written before 2 Peter and that the writer of 2 Peter used Jude as a source. The issues addressed in these two documents are so similar that when we consider Jude, we also open a window on 2 Peter. Indeed, the two books put forward essentially the same messages by warning their communities not to follow false teachers (Jude 3–4, 7–8, 10, 12–13, 16, 18–19; 2 Pet 2:1–3, 10b–22).

With respect to our ongoing search for how the biblical writers portray punishment, especially punishment in the afterlife, we note that Jude 14–15 directly cites the book of Enoch (discussed in chap. 2) in saying that God is coming with a host of angels to pass judgment on "all" with a particular eye on convicting all the ungodly (1 En. 1.9). The punishment Enoch has in mind, as we know from our previous discussion, is prolonged life in flames. When Jude and 2 Peter refer to condemnation because of the congregation's sin, they have punishment by fire in mind.

Jude and 2 Peter warn the congregations to avoid false teachers so that listeners will not fall under the same judgment as the teachers. The false teachers have already been condemned (Jude 4; 2 Pet 2:3). To underscore the importance of avoiding the false teachers, Jude and 2 Peter set out lists of those whom God destroyed because they were not faithful. God did not spare the angels who sinned (Gen 6:1–4) but kept them "in eternal chains in deepest darkness for the judgment of the great day" (Jude 6). In 2 Peter 2:4, the NRSVue says that God cast the angels into "hell," which is here not the word "Gehenna" but a form of the word "Tartarus," which in Greek mythology was an abyss where some of the gods locked their prisoners.

A list of similar cases follows. Sodom and Gomorrah (Gen 19) are a prime example as they are punished by "eternal fire" (Jude 7; 2 Pet 2:6–10). Jude 11–13 cites Cain (Gen 4), Balaam (Num 22–24), and Korah (Num 16) as examples of those whose sin God remembered and punished. Balaam "was rebuked for his own transgression; a speechless donkey spoke with a human voice and restrained the prophet's madness" (2 Pet 2:16). God "knows how to . . . keep the unrighteous until the day of judgment, when they will be punished" (2 Pet 2:9).

The punishment set out in the book of Enoch awaits those in the time of Jude who, in the grip of the false teachers, scoff, indulge in their own "ungodly lusts," are "devoid of the Spirit," and cause division (Jude 18–19). Second Peter is even more explicit:

> The present heavens and earth have been reserved for fire, being kept until the day of judgment and destruction of the godless.... The day of the Lord will come like a thief, and then the heavens will pass away with a loud noise, and the elements will be destroyed with fire, and the earth and everything that is done on it will be disclosed. (2 Pet 3:7, 10; cf. 3:11–13)

Given this mode of punishment, Jude's admonition to snatch the unfaithful "out of the fire" (Jude 23) is more than a metaphor.

The Book of Revelation

The book of Revelation is the fullest expression of end-time literature in the Bible. The writer is identified as John (Rev 1:1–2) but is not likely the author of the Gospel and Letters of John. This John, the author of Revelation, who is also known as John of Patmos, believed that the last days were under way and that many in the churches needed to repent in expectation of the final judgment. John expected the destruction of the present world and the creation of a new heaven and earth to occur "soon" (e.g., Rev 1:1; 22:20), although he does not speculate on a more precise date. The important thing to note is that the time for God's wrath has come (e.g., 6:17; 11:18). John wrote to encourage followers of Jesus to remain faithful even as their conflict with the Roman Empire intensified, so that when God made the final judgment, they could become part of the new world. Repentance was for some (e.g., 2:1–3:22).

According to John, God would punish the Roman Empire and those who shared its values and practices in two stages—present and future (final). In Revelation 13:10, John employs the device we mentioned in connection with Paul to say that God was already at work punishing the empire and its inhabitants through the means by which they sinned; the false values, exploitation, and violence that characterized Roman rule were leading to the fall of the empire. This theme permeates the book of Revelation—for example, in the opening of the six seals (6:1–17), the blowing of the seven trumpets (8:6–11:19), and the pouring of the seven bowls of wrath (16:1–21).

While punishment is already under way through painful social developments, a final judgment is coming. John envisions this occasion as a fierce battle between God and Satan and their respective forces (Rev 19:11–21). After the battle, God consigns Satan and the religious leaders who facilitated the practice of the empire "into the lake of fire that burns with sulfur" (19:20). This, however, is a temporary state of affairs. God places the captives in a bottomless pit where they wait for a thousand years, often called the millennium, while Jesus and the martyrs reign over the world (20:1–6). After that God releases Satan and allows Satan to try to deceive the earth again. However, God defeats this enemy and his entourage (20:7–9). God throws the devil into "the lake of fire and sulfur" (to join the beast and the false prophet), where "they will be tormented day and night forever and ever" (20:10).

After that, God holds the Last Judgment. The dead are raised and stand before the throne. The sea gives up its dead, as do Death and Hades. The deeds of the dead have been recorded in books, and they are judged on the basis of "their works, as recorded in the books . . . according to what they had done. Then Death and Hades were thrown into the lake of fire. This is the second death, the lake of fire, and anyone whose name was not found written in the book of life was thrown into the lake of fire" (20:12–15). In the coming world, there is no place for Death or for Hades, which John likely views in a traditional way as a repository for the dead.

Because Revelation uses so many images to convey meaning, some interpreters think that its author does not intend to refer to a literal lake of fire but uses the language of fire to invoke the notion of separation from God. Even if that is the case, the image of God casting beings into the fire bespeaks God actively punishing the disobedient, presumably "forever and ever."

The Gospel and Letters of John

The author of the Gospel and Letters of John views existence as taking place in two spheres rather like a two-story house. Reminiscent of some of the philosophers of the period, especially Jewish thinkers who had been influenced significantly by Greek thought, this John envisions an upper story (heaven) and a lower story (the world). Heaven is the sphere where God dwells and is marked by qualities such as life, love, truth, and sight (the capacity to perceive the truth). By contrast, the world is a sphere marked by such things as death, hate, falsehood, and blindness (being unable or unwilling to perceive the truth).

With respect to eternal life and condemnation, the Fourth Gospel concentrates on what happens in the present. Scholars refer to this phenomenon as realized eschatology. For those who believe in Jesus, "eternal life" begins in the present (e.g., John 5:28; 11:25). Eternal life begins with experiencing the qualities of heaven while one is still in the world and becomes complete when Jesus takes believers into heaven (14:1–4). John speaks plainly about the fate of those who do not believe in Jesus: "Those who do not believe are condemned already because they have not believed in the name of the only Son of God. And this is the judgment, that the light has come into the world, and people loved darkness rather than light" (3:18–19). Like eternal life, condemnation is already at work in the present among those who do not believe. "The ruler of this world" (the devil) while still existing is also already condemned (12:31; 16:11). Indeed, Jesus says, "I have much to condemn" (8:26). Condemnation in the present is continuing to experience the negative qualities of the world as if there is no alternative.

John does anticipate a "last day" (5:28; 6:39–40, 44, 54), that is, an end to present existence, but does not give much attention to how or when this will take place. John is concerned with what will happen to believers and nonbelievers at that point. Jesus will usher believers into heaven, where their eternal life will continue without interference from the world. The last day will bring a final condemnation (5:29).

While John does not give much attention to what will happen to nonbelievers after the last day, one of the most beloved verses in the Bible offers a clue: "For God so loved the world that [God] gave [God's] only Son, so that everyone who believes in him may not *perish* but may have eternal life" (3:16; our emphasis). The Fourth Gospel does not elaborate on what it means to perish (Gk. *apollymi*). But John seems to use this word in the sense of "go out of existence," as when Jesus instructs the disciples to gather up the crumbs after the feeding of the five thousand "so that nothing may be lost" (John 6:12; cf. 6:27). The food that is "lost" decays and goes out of existence. To "perish" evidently means to go out of existence.

The Book of Hebrews

The document known as To the Hebrews is probably the first fully developed Christian sermon in existence. For this writer, every transgression deserves "a just penalty" (Heb 2:2). While God makes it possible for Jesus to lead "many children to glory" (2:10) and thereby avoid penalty, those who follow Jesus must be faithful and must hold firm (3:19). Those who do not endure will not enter God's rest; that is, they will not make the journey to heaven (3:6; 18; 4:6; 10:26–31). Believers will render an account to God to determine whether they can enter God's rest (4:13). It is difficult for those who once believed and were faithful but have fallen away to inherit the promise (6:1–8). After mortals have died, "the judgment" follows (9:27). The writer speaks vividly in saying that the judgment is "a fearful prospect" and will be "a fury of fire that will consume the adversaries," asking, "How much worse punishment do you think will be deserved by those who have spurned the Son of God?" (10:27, 29; cf. 12:25–27). However, those who accept the discipline of God will receive "the peaceful fruit of righteousness" (12:11). Discipline requires following the example of the leaders in faith (11:4–38) and especially enduring suffering as Jesus did (12:1–12). Only thus can the congregation avoid punishment and become a part of the dominion "that cannot be shaken" (12:28).

On the subject of punishment in the afterlife, the New Testament contains diverse viewpoints. Christians should not speak simply of *the* New Testament understanding of hell. Rather, when drawing on the New Testament writers, we need to take into account the particular perceptions of hell associated with different writers and books. Interpreters need to respect the otherness of the individual writers. By honoring the integrity of the particularity of each writer, the interpreting community will then be in a good position to identify those aspects of the text that are theologically appealing and those that raise questions or hesitation.

Part 2

Voices on Hell from the History of the Church

Part 2 considers how views of hell developed in the history of the church after the biblical period into the late nineteenth century. Chapter 4 reaches from the second century to the Reformation in the late 1500s and early 1600s. Chapter 5 picks up the story from the Reformation to the late 1800s and early 1900s.

Chapter 4

Voices from the Second Century CE to the Reformation

*T*he concept of hell along with apocalyptic theologies emerged late in the Second Temple period of ancient Judaism. First-century Christians picked up and passed on these ideas, as seen in the New Testament, ideas that were developed further during the centuries that followed. While belief in eternal punishment and hell were passed on through time, these beliefs were not monolithic. In this chapter, we explore the concept of hell and its alternatives, beginning in the second century and concluding with the eve of the Reformation. We take up perspectives developed during the Reformation and afterward in chapter 5. As we move through time, we'll see that these beliefs did not arise in a vacuum but reflected inheritances from the biblical story as well as other cultural influences, including Greco-Roman ideas. We need to remember that Christianity developed over several centuries as a persecuted, minority sect that achieved toleration and then official status only in the fourth century CE.

Eternal Punishment in Early Christianity

References to hell, Hades, or Gehenna in the second century are present in the writings of the church but are generally few in number. When they appear, they typically reflect responses to martyrdom or persecution. Thus Polycarp, who was executed by the Roman government in the middle of the second century, is reported to have said, "The fire you threaten burns but an hour and is quenched after a little; for you do not know the fire of the coming judgment and everlasting punishment that is laid up for the impious. But why do you delay? Come, do what you will."[1] Justin Martyr, writing in defense of the Christian faith in a hostile culture that assumed some form of eternal punishment for the wicked, mentions Gehenna and eternal punishment in his *First Apology,* but it is not a dominant theme. Drawing on Luke 12:4–5, he does note that "Gehenna is the place where those who live unrighteously will be punished and those who do not believe that these things will come to pass which God has taught through Christ." Justin offers a more detailed picture in responding to those who react to the gospel with hostility by seeking to kill Christians; they will face "eternal punishment through fire."[2]

A more detailed picture of eternal punishment and the idea of hell is found in apocalyptic works such as the second-century Apocalypse of Peter, which was seen by some as canonical at least until the fourth century. The picture painted in this work is important because it proved to be influential in Dante's vision of hell, which is influential to this day. While we do not have a complete version of this apocalypse, we know from early Christian writers that it was highly regarded. It depicts hell as a place of eternal punishment in graphic terms. The nature of the punishments reflects the alleged wickedness of the individual being punished. For example, the author pictures women judged to be adulterers being hung by their hair above a boiling mire or swamp, while male adulterers are hung by their feet, with their heads hidden in the mire. Murderers are cast into a place filled with evil creeping things, such as worms, that prey upon them. The rich who ignore widows and orphans are sent to a place marked by "gravel-stones sharper than swords or any spit, heated with fire, and men and women clad in filthy rags rolled upon them in torment." In other words, people consigned to hell reap what they had sown in life.[3]

As with the emergence of visions of postmortem punishment in ancient Judaism, the presence of such ideas in early Christianity was often related to experiences of persecution. We already saw an example in the Martyrdom of Polycarp. In the third century, Cyprian of Carthage addresses a period of severe persecution, writing in detail about eternal punishment in hell (Gehenna) being meted out against the persecutors. He encourages the people to embrace martyrdom with the promise of reward for the faithful and punishment for the persecutor: "Oh, what and how great will that day be at its coming, beloved brethren, when the Lord shall begin to count up His people, . . . to send the guilty to Gehenna, and to set on fire our persecutors with the perpetual burning of a penal fire, but to pay to us the reward of our faith and devotion!" (Epistle 55:10).[4] In *An Address to Demetrianus,* Cyprian writes that "an ever-burning Gehenna will burn up the condemned, and a punishment devouring with living flames." This torment will continue without end, such that those who persecuted the church will be "compensated by a perpetual spectacle, according to the truth of Holy Scripture, which says, 'Their worm shall not die, and their fire shall not be quenched; and they shall be for a vision to all flesh.'"[5] While Cyprian sought to encourage fellow Christians by promising eternal punishment for the persecutor, such threats of eternal punishment had evangelistic dimensions as well, since preachers could urge listeners to avoid punishment by embracing Christ and being faithful to him.

After Christianity became a licit and then official religion in the Roman Empire in the fourth century CE, the targets of judgment, hell, and eternal punishment moved from persecutors to heretics and other ecclesiastical offenders. While the Apocalypse of Peter faded from view, a new apocalyptic text, the Apocalypse of Paul, emerged. Though it is similar in its descriptions of hell's torments, it turns from focusing on pagan persecutors and idolaters to slack Christians, unruly church officers, and heretics.[6] As Bart Ehrman points out, in the age of Theodosius at the end of the fourth century, when Christianity is the religion of the state, "Pagan cults are suffering; pagan numbers are shrinking; Christianity is strong, influential, and growing by leaps and bounds. The 'pagan problem' is scarcely a problem at all, and so the author's attention has turned elsewhere—to the burgeoning but problem-ridden Christian community itself."[7] The threat of hell is intended to keep an expanding Christian community in line. While Augustine and other scholars of the day rejected the authenticity of the Apocalypse of Paul, it remained popular through the medieval age until Dante wrote the *Divine Comedy.* Alan Bernstein writes that "Dante had only to add conversations with the damned to adapt this structure for the *Divine Comedy.*"[8]

Alternatives to Eternal Punishment in Hell

While some early Christian writers began to develop the idea of eternal punishment, often in some form of hell, alternatives were proposed, at least in terms of the length of time in hell. Foremost among those who proposed such alternatives was Origen of Alexandria (185–254 CE). He envisioned the possibility that all might experience salvation as part of the restoration of all things (Gk. *apokatastasis*). While Origen's views would be condemned in the sixth century, his influence would live on through Eastern theologians such as Gregory of Nyssa (fourth century CE).

Origen did not reject the idea of postmortem punishment, but he believed such punishment should be corrective and not permanent. The point of such punishment was to eliminate the condition that led to punishment. In essence, he envisioned a form of purgation or refinement so that a person might be reunited with God.[9] In his *Contra Celsum,* Origen distinguishes between Sheol/Hades and Gehenna. The former was where the dead resided until Jesus descended into Hades in what is known as the "harrowing of hell," an event that he believed was hinted at in 1 Peter 4:6. Origen speaks of Jesus' visit as a bodiless soul to preach to those in Sheol/Hades so they might believe (*Cels*. 2.43).[10] As for Gehenna, Origen envisioned it as a place of torment, but again he did not believe it would be a permanent condition. The goal of hell is the destruction of evil, so that the person might be restored (*Cels*. 8.72).[11] Because Origen's writings were condemned by a church council in the sixth century, much of his writings are either lost or corrupted by later translators and opponents.

One question raised concerning Origen's beliefs was whether he envisioned the restoration of Satan, because the message that evil will not persist to the end could involve the restoration of Satan or Satan's annihilation. The challenge of interpreting Origen is that he often engaged in speculation. It should be noted that those who followed Origen, such as Gregory of Nyssa, did not believe that Satan would be restored.

Gregory of Nyssa, a fourth-century Cappadocian bishop and theologian, followed Origen in many ways. When it comes to Hades, he interpreted it in more spiritual terms. He writes that considering the different parts of the narrative in the parable of Lazarus and the rich man (Luke 16:19-31), Hades "is not intended to signify a place with that name. The Scripture must be teaching us that it is some invisible and incorporeal condition of life, in which the soul lives."[12] As far as the purgation of evil and the reason it can be painful for the soul, Gregory writes, using the refining of gold as an analogy, so that "when evil is consumed by the purifying fire, the soul, which is united to evil must necessarily be in the fire until the base adulterant material is removed, consumed by the fire." He also uses the analogy of removing mud from a rope. When it comes to the soul, "wrapped up as it is in material and earthly attachments, it struggles and is stretched, as God draws His own to Himself. What is alien to God has to be scraped off forcibly because it has somehow grown onto the soul. This is the cause of the sharp and unbearable pains which the soul must endure."[13]

Of course, not all Eastern Christians embraced universalism, the idea that everyone will be saved. For example, Augustine's contemporary John Chrysostom (347–407) argues against the doctrine of universal restoration. He asks about the justice of the righteous enjoying the same lot as sinners; in his mind, "Such a confusion as this even man would not make, much less God! But if you will, I will show you that even in the case of sinners, arguing from existing facts, there is this distinction, and exact just judgment."[14] In his *Third Homily on Philemon* he writes, "That there will, then, be a hell, we have, as I think, sufficiently proved, bringing forward the deluge, and former evils, and arguing that it is not possible that He who performed these things should leave the men of the present age unpunished."[15]

John of Damascus (655–740) also affirms a doctrine of hell but does not go into detail, as seen in this word from *Against the Manichaeans*:

> After death, there is no means for repentance, not because God does not accept repentance—He cannot deny Himself nor lose His compassion—but the soul does not change anymore . . . people after death are unchangeable, so that on the one hand the righteous desire God and always have Him to rejoice in, while sinners desire sin though they do not have the material

means to sin . . . they are punished without any consolation. For what is hell but the deprivation of that which is exceedingly desired by someone? Therefore, according to the analogy of desire, whoever desires God rejoices and whoever desires sin is punished.[16]

If these two Eastern theologians argued on behalf of hell, even if not focusing on either its eternity or its nature, Maximus the Confessor (580–662) was open to the idea of universal restoration. However, after the condemnations of Origen at the Fifth Ecumenical Council at Constantinople (543), which took place at the behest of Justinian, the eastern Roman emperor, he had to be cautious in his advocacy of the doctrine of *apokatastasis*. Nevertheless, following Gregory of Nyssa, he writes in his answer to Question 19 of his *Questions and Doubts* that the church knew three restorations (*apokatastasis*). It is the third restoration that is of importance here. That form is "the restoration of the powers of the soul that fell into sin, returning to that for which they were created." Thus, through the resurrection, the "distorted powers of the soul in the duration of the ages again throw off the memories of evil lodged within it and passing through all ages, and not finding a resting place, return to God, who is without limit."[17] While he does not mention hell or judgment in this passage, in other passages in his works he speaks of eternal separation from God. He believed that it was God's goal in history for all of humanity, indeed all of creation, to experience union with God. However, he could also envision humans frustrating God's saving purpose. Thus, Maximus might offer hope of universal salvation, but we must be cautious in making that claim, since he also spoke of judgment in terms of eternal separation from God.[18]

Jumping forward to the seventh century, the Syriac bishop Isaac of Nineveh (613–c. 700), a theologian recognized as a saint by the Assyrian Church of the East, suggests that terms like wrath, anger, and hatred when used for the Creator should be seen figuratively, for they do not describe God's true identity. Therefore, when it comes to Gehenna, the purpose of being sentenced to that place is to bring perfection to our actions. Ultimately, Isaac understands the world to come in terms of "grace, love, mercy, and goodness, and because the resurrection from the dead is also a demonstration of the mercifulness of God and of the overflowing abundance of His love which cannot be repaid, how (can one think of) a dispensation in which are included requitals for our own good or evil (actions)?" So, Gehenna is understood in terms of divine mercy due to God's eternal goodness, so that all might be restored.[19]

If Cyprian envisions a hellish future for those who persecuted Christians and the Apocalypse of Paul applies that punishment to ecclesiastical offenders, Origen, Gregory of Nyssa, Maximus the Confessor, and Isaac of Nineveh envision Hades and Gehenna either as temporary existences or a spiritual existence (with both ideas being influenced by Platonism, with its idea of heaven above and the earth below, and the goal of the soul being to journey from the earth to heaven).

Augustine and Eternal Punishment in the Western Church

When it comes to the foundations for understanding the concept of eternal punishment in the later Western church, the key figure is Augustine. The primary sources of material on this matter are found in *The City of God* and *The Enchiridion*. While *The Enchiridion* served as a compendium of Augustine's teachings, *The City of God,* written after Alaric's sack of Rome in 410, in part was a response to pagan charges that Alaric's sacking of Rome was due to Rome's abandonment of the Roman gods. Augustine responds to this charge by suggesting that Rome had experienced a false prosperity, and that life was to be understood as a struggle between good and evil, with the Last Judgment leading to one of two destinations, heaven or hell. The consequences of that judgment were permanent.

Augustine's view of history, unlike the cyclical view of history espoused by Origen, was linear. Thus, unlike Origen, he did not allow for postmortem correction leading to salvation. When it came to the purgation of sin/evil, Augustine assumed that it applied only to believers requiring cleansing, not postmortem salvation. He envisioned two deaths, with the first being an individual's death, and the second taking place after the general resurrection that leads to judgment day. During the interim period, a soul exists in "hidden retreat, where it enjoys rest or suffers affliction just in proportion to the merit it has earned by the life which it led on earth."[20] After the general resurrection and Last Judgment, a soul would be consigned to one of two kingdoms, that of God or that of the devil. At this point, one's future is fixed. The good go to the kingdom of God and the wicked to the devil's kingdom, where they experience a "miserable existence in eternal death without the power of dying." While the good experience a happy existence, the wicked experience "degrees of misery, one being more endurably miserable than another."[21] While punishment is present in the kingdom of the devil, perhaps more important is the perpetual "alienation from the life of God."[22] As for those who complain about these matters, Augustine simply points to Scripture that speaks of both God's mercy and God's wrath. When it comes to the question of whether the fire involved would consume the body of the person consigned to hell and thus annihilate it, Augustine answers that everyone receives a resurrection body that is of a different substance that cannot be consumed, even by the fires of hell.[23]

Augustine does not focus on the gore of eternal punishment, as do the Apocalypse of Peter and the Apocalypse of Paul, the latter of which he considered nothing more than fables. Instead, he chose to offer a more intellectually focused argument. It provided a foundation for what was to come in the Western church.

Medieval Visions of Hell

Augustine serves as a turning point between early Christianity and the medieval church, at least in the Latin West. Origen's vision of the restoration of all things was condemned under Justinian at the Fifth Ecumenical Council held at Constantinople in 553, which led to the destruction of his Greek texts. At that council, it was decreed that "if anyone says or holds that the punishment of devils and wicked men is temporary and will eventually cease, that is to say, that devils or the ungodly will be completely restored to their original state: let him be anathema."[24] While Origen's ideas were condemned, they would be reinterpreted by persons such as

Gregory of Nyssa and would persist in the East. As for the Western church, Augustine's vision provided the foundation for common beliefs about hell and eternal punishment.

Most medieval Christians, following Augustine, assumed human beings were infected with original sin, which by itself warrants condemnation to hell. Grace serves as the foundation for salvation, but three things are necessary if grace is to be sustained: faith, sacraments, and good works. Baptism is the foundation piece because it washes away original sin. From there penance is a necessary step in taking care of the effects of one's mortal (deadly) and venial (pardonable) sins. The idea of purgatory emerged in the medieval era as a way for forgivable sins to be answered for after death when satisfaction (the final step of penance) had not been completed in one's lifetime.

Moving forward in time, we encounter Pope Gregory the Great (c. 540–604). As with Augustine, Gregory understood hell to be eternal in duration and involve torturous punishment that corresponds to one's sins. The location of hell is subterranean, with the volcanoes in Sicily providing portals to it. As Alan Bernstein details in his examination of Gregory's views, Gregory drew on both theology and folklore to communicate his perspective on hell, which is both doctrinal and pastoral, the latter focusing on encouraging proper behavior. In two works, *Dialogues* and *Moralia,* Gregory goes into great detail, seeking to answer questions regarding judgment and hell, including the possibility of purgatory, such that some sins might be forgiven after death but before the final judgment. While Gregory sees the teachings on judgment and hell serving as an incentive to behavioral change, he also understands it in terms of theodicy (defense of God in the face of evil). In his view, continued perversity deserves punishment. It is a matter of justice if one will not change. In *Moralia,* Gregory writes:

> The wicked end their iniquities because they end their lives. Indeed, they would have wished to live without end so that they would have been able to persist in their iniquities. For they prefer to sin more than to live and therefore they desire to live here forever so that they would never leave off sinning as

long as they live. It pertains to the justice of the strict and just Judge that no one whose mind ever wished to lack sin in this life should ever lack punishment, and that no end of vengeance is given to the wicked person, because, for as long as he was able, he did not wish to have an end to crime."[25]

Several centuries later, Hugh of St. Victor (1096–1141) spoke of hell in similar terms, suggesting that it is "the place of those who are confirmed in evil and who have irrecoverably forsaken discipline, and accordingly evil only and the supreme evil is placed there." Hugh understood purgatory to be the middle place between hell and heaven, from which one "could ascend through the merit of righteousness or descend through the guilt of sin."[26]

The most important theologian of the Middle Ages was Thomas Aquinas (1225–74); his perspective on hell would influence later medieval thinking, even if Dante's *Divine Comedy* was the most influential work on a popular level. Thomas taught that after death the body is separated from the soul, "and since a place is assigned to souls in keeping with their reward or punishment, as soon as the soul is set free from the body it is either plunged into hell or soars to heaven, unless it be held back by some debt, for which its flight must needs be delayed until the soul is first of all cleansed."[27] This last destination is a reference to purgatory. When it comes to the geography of hell (Lat. *infernus*), Thomas speaks in terms of a four-level subterranean dungeon. Hell proper lay at the bottom of the four levels. It was a place where the damned perpetually suffered torment. Those who dwelled at this level experienced both pain and the loss of sight of God. Above it stood the level where unbaptized children were housed ("limbo of infants"). They suffered only from the loss of sight of God. Above this level was a place of temporary torment and suffering, also known as purgatory. While those housed at this level lost sight of God and experienced suffering, they did not lose grace and thus could be rescued on the day of judgment, if not before. This served as a place where the saints in need of purification received that refining fire. Finally, the top level was the holding place for the saints of the Old Testament ("limbo of the fathers"). This is, according to Thomas, the level of hell visited by Jesus between Good Friday and Easter morning, freeing these saints from limbo.[28]

As Augustine did, Thomas Aquinas taught that there would be two resurrections, the last being the general resurrection leading to the Last Judgment. Divine judgment led to corporeal punishment, including suffering from fire and worms. More importantly for our purposes, Thomas addresses in the *Supplement to the Summa* the justice of eternal punishment, such that "according to Divine justice, sin renders a person worthy to be altogether cut off from the fellowship of God's city, and this is the effect of every sin committed against charity, which is the bond uniting this same city together." Therefore, when it comes to mortal sin, one is expelled forever and condemned to eternal punishment. Again, this is in accord with God's justice. It also accords with God's mercy:

> God, for His own part, has mercy on all. Since, however, His mercy is ruled by the order of His wisdom, the result is that it does not reach to certain people who render themselves unworthy of that mercy, as do the demons and the damned who are obstinate in wickedness. And yet we may say that even in them His mercy finds a place, in so far as they are punished less than they deserve condignly, but not that they are entirely delivered from punishment.[29]

For Thomas, mortal sin results in being sentenced to the fourth level of hell, where there is no hope of escape.

By the twelfth and thirteenth centuries, purgatory had become an important part of the conversation. As we see with Thomas, it is a form of punishment, but with a corrective element, such that the suffering is not permanent. Thomas believed that one could and should pray for those experiencing purgatory, that they might be released from their sins. One need not pray for the saints in heaven, as they are already fully cleansed, nor for those in hell, for they are beyond hope. Purgatory offers a third means of experiencing restoration after death. Regarding the geography of purgatory and hell, Thomas assumes they are near each other so that both experience the same fire. However, the one in purgatory is farther from the fire and will not endure it forever. So, he writes in response to objections to his view: "The punishment of hell is for the purpose of affliction, wherefore it is called by the names of things that are wont to afflict us here. But the chief purpose of the punishment of Purgatory is to cleanse us from the remains of sin; and consequently the pain of fire only is ascribed to Purgatory, because fire cleanses and consumes."[30] More will be said about purgatory in later chapters.

Since Thomas Aquinas was a Dominican theologian, it is worth noting that a fellow Dominican, Humbert of Romans, in his *Treatise on the Formation of Preachers*, connected the importance of preaching to the problem of hell. He noted that preachers could address the problem of hell filling up by making known knowledge of the word of God. Without preaching, hearts will not be stirred toward heavenly blessings. He writes that it is "supremely necessary for the barbarian peoples of the world to come to faith in Christ because without it they cannot be saved." Following Paul in Romans 10, he asks how one can hear without preaching and concludes:

> From all of this we can see how necessary the job of preaching is. Without it the fulness of glory of the kingdom of heaven will not be realized, *without it Hell would be filled more quickly and the world would be altogether barren;* the demons would prevail in the world, the hearts of men would not rise up to hope for heaven, the peoples of the world would not have received the Christian faith, and the church would not have been founded or made progress, nor would she be able to stand.[31]

For many medieval Christians, hell was a place to be feared and avoided. It was not seen by most Western Christian theologians as contrary to God's love and mercy, but rather as an expression of God's justice. As Humbert taught, preaching could help alleviate the problem of hell, if people respond to the invitation.

While in the West we see few alternatives to hell that would either limit time or allow for escape, attempts were made to distinguish the levels of punishment. In essence, the punishment was to fit the crime. There were also suggestions that one might experience a respite from the punishment present in hell, thus softening the nature of hell's oppressiveness. Concern about the nature of punishment also led to the development of the concept of purgatory, even if it took place before the Last Judgment. There were even stories of rescues from hell, in addition to the story of Jesus' harrowing of hell during the interregnum between his death and resurrection.[32]

Dante's Legacy

When we envision hell, much of the imagery is rooted in Dante Alighieri's (1265–1321) epic *The Divine Comedy,* which takes us on a pilgrimage in the company of the Roman poet Virgil to hell, purgatory, and finally paradise. As we conclude this chapter, we want to acknowledge Dante's legacy, especially that of *The Inferno.* The primary influences on Dante's vision are Virgil's *Aeneid* and Thomas Aquinas's *Summa theologica,* though there are similarities to earlier apocalyptic works, including the Apocalypse of Peter and the Apocalypse of Paul.

The first of the three sections of Dante's *Divine Comedy,* the one we focus on here, is *Inferno* (hell). It was likely completed around 1314. The book as a whole tells the story of a journey that a pilgrim (a fictional version of Dante) takes in the company of Virgil (reason) at the behest of Beatrice (divine revelation) through hell and purgatory to salvation (paradise). The message is that what God does for the pilgrim, God can do for everyone. Seeking to escape from the Dark Wood, he must go down into hell before climbing up toward paradise and salvation. The message is that this journey is necessary because one must understand sin (fraud, violence, and concupiscence) before experiencing salvation. Between hell and paradise lies purgatory, a place of repentance, regeneration, and conversion.

In Dante's vision, hell is a place of pain, suffering, and torment. As the pilgrim enters hell, he encounters a sign above a ledge: "Before me, nothing but eternal things were made, and I shall last eternally. Abandon every hope, all you who enter" (*Inferno* 3.9).[33] For Dante, following Thomas Aquinas's view of the moral good, people experience the suffering of hell because they have chosen to live immoral lives. As Eleonore Stump writes, "So what God has on his hands in the case of those who eventually end up in Dante's hell is persons who *will* not will what they need to will in order for God to be able to unite them to himself in heaven and who by their repeated irrational choices violating their nature have produced in themselves a second, vicious nature. It is not possible for God to bring such persons to heaven." God could annihilate the wicked, but for Thomas that would be an evil act.[34] Dante creates a vision of a place where the wicked can no longer do evil but also cannot experience any further decay. While the punishment is understood to fit the crime,

> Dante does not present hell as God's torture chamber in which the damned shriek insanely to eternity under the torments imposed by God. In the case of Filippo Argenti, a wealthy member of Florentine society and enemy of Dante, it hardly seems true to say that his pains are imposed by God at all, for what Filippo suffers by way of physical pain is largely a result of what his companions in the Styx do to him and what he does to himself. Filippo's punishment is in a sense a natural consequence of the way he chooses to act.[35]

While we think of hell in terms of fire, it should be noted that the ninth circle, the bottom circle, is frozen. In the last canto of the *Inferno,* Lucifer/Satan stands in a lake frozen to his waist. This version of Lucifer is a giant with three heads, and in each mouth is one of three of the greatest traitors, Judas Iscariot, Brutus, and Cassius. Dante and Virgil escape hell to purgatory by climbing down Lucifer's frozen and hairy body, and then out of the cavern they travel to purgatory (canto 34).

From here we turn to the Reformation and beyond. Visions of hell that we've seen to this point reflect cultural dynamics. Moderns might find some of the imagery and the theology uncomfortable and even appalling. While alternatives were suggested, they were generally from minority voices.

Chapter 5

Voices from the Reformation to the Twentieth Century

*W*e leave behind Dante's poetic and at times horrific picture of hell as found in the *Inferno,* book 1 of his *Divine Comedy,* and find ourselves in the sixteenth century. It is a period of turmoil and change that has been under way for some time. The church in the West is seen by many as corrupt. The Renaissance popes were known more for their worldliness than their piety. Consider Pope Julius II (died in 1513), known as the Warrior Pope, who is thought to have chosen Julius as his papal name in honor of Julius Caesar. His successor, Leo X, issued indulgences to finance the construction of St. Peter's, which got the attention of Martin Luther in 1517. The church in western Europe was at a breaking point; the resulting Reformation split Western Christendom into rival factions, Protestant and Catholic. While they differed in many respects, when it came to the question of hell they were largely on the same page. The one major difference was that the Reformers rejected purgatory, leaving two options for the afterlife, heaven and hell. What marked most of the Reformers was their embrace of Augustine, turning aside many theological developments that had emerged in the millennium that separated them from Augustine. It was understood that hell was a place created by God for the eternal punishment of the wicked.

Reformation-Era Developments

We might start with a noted scholar who shared many concerns with Martin Luther and other Reformers, but who chose not to jump ship. That would be Desiderius Erasmus of Rotterdam (c. 1466–1536), who desired a return to a more biblical form of Christianity. He used his famed book *In Praise of Folly* (1511) to satirize the medieval church. Erasmus embraced Plato over Aristotle and complained about indulgences, masses for the dead, and the provision of financial means of salvation. He seemed bemused by the interest of theologians of the past and present in the idea of hell. Thus he writes: "Then for what concerns hell, how exactly they describe everything, as if they had been conversant in that commonwealth the most part of their time!"[1] While he shows little interest in the subject, there is also little or no evidence that he ever questioned the existence of hell or its eternity, even if he admired Origen.

We mention Erasmus because he was a leading humanist thinker who shared some concerns about the Roman Catholic Church and scholastic theology with what came to be the Protestant Reformers. The major Reformers, beginning with Martin Luther, allow for only two destinations after death: heaven and hell. While hell played a role in the theology of the Reformers, it wasn't a central concern. Hell served as a warning of the dangers of sin to one's eternal destiny, but according to Luther, one's eternal destiny is in the hands of God, and good works do not contribute to one's destiny.

Like Erasmus, Luther was critical of the church leadership and scholastic theology, but unlike Erasmus, he left (or was forced out of) the Catholic Church. Personality played a major role in the differences between the two men. There is no doubt that Luther affirmed the traditional view of hell, though he drew his understanding of hell from Augustine and not Thomas Aquinas. Luther's view of salvation was rooted in his belief that God alone elected persons to salvation or damnation, a perspective on predestination he drew from Augustine. In formulating his vision of judgment, he rejected purgatory as an option, simply leaving heaven and hell. As Alice Turner notes, Luther's "Hell was Augustine's, dire and eternal, constructed by an omnipotent God to punish the wicked. No one would be saved but by God's grace, and there was no way to influence the outcome."[2] Good works could not influence God's choice in the matter, nor could prayers for the dead. Nevertheless, in a sermon from 1519 on preparing to die, Luther encourages his listeners not to be concerned about whether or not one is consigned to hell: "You must not regard hell and eternal pain in relation to predestination, not in yourself, or in itself, or in those who are damned, nor must you be worried by the many people in the world who are not chosen. If you are not careful, that picture will quickly upset you and be your downfall."[3] In other words, leave things in God's hands, because you cannot change what cannot be changed.

Not long after Luther broke with the Roman Catholic Church over indulgences and other matters, including purgatory, reform broke out in Zurich, Switzerland, led by Ulrich Zwingli (1484–1531). Zwingli was more influenced by humanism than Luther, but he came out in a similar place on the question of purgatory and hell. Regarding purgatory, he wrote in his *Exposition of the Faith:*

> Inasmuch as Christ himself taught that those who believe in him have eternal life, and that those who believe in him that sent him will not come into condemnation but have already passed from death to life, it is manifest that the period of purgatorial torment laid by the papists upon the souls of those who depart this life is a figment of their own invention.[4]

Although Zwingli is considered to be the first Swiss reformer, and thus a fountain of the Reformed tradition, John Calvin has been more influential in the longer term.

As did Luther and Zwingli, Calvin affirmed the reality of hell (Gehenna) but did not focus on it. His only reference to hell in the *Institutes of the Christian Religion* notes that "no description can deal adequately with the gravity of God's vengeance against the wicked." Therefore, Calvin uses images such as weeping, gnashing of teeth, and unquenchable fire to help people "conceive the lot of the wicked, so we ought especially fix our thoughts upon this: how wretched it is to be cut off from all fellowship with God" (*Institutes* 3.25.12).[5] Where Calvin went beyond Luther was in pushing his doctrine of predestination much further. Calvin taught a version of predestination known as double predestination: God not only chooses who will receive salvation but also predetermines who will be condemned to hell. Therefore, as Alice Turner notes, for Calvin, "prayers, good works, deathbed repentances, and absolutions cannot change inexorable fate." While Calvin admitted that his doctrine of double predestination was harsh, "nevertheless, it was a logically consistent position, given God's all-knowing omnipotence."[6] Considering Calvin's background in the law, it is not surprising that he would seek to be consistent in his teachings on last things. Therefore, in terms of Christ's act of atonement for human sin, he died only for the elect.

For Luther, Zwingli, and Calvin, following Augustine, and purportedly Paul, the assumption is that all humanity is dead in their sins because of the fall of Adam and Eve. All deserve condemnation (hell); by God's grace some are saved, but not because of works or merit. Such grace and mercy from God are received by faith in Christ. Calvin was very explicit when it came to who was to be counted among the elect and who was not: "As Scripture, then, clearly shows, we say that God once established by his eternal and unchangeable plan those whom he long before determined once for all to receive into salvation, and those whom, on the other hand, he would devote to destruction" (*Institutes* 3.21.7).

We spoke first of the three primary Reformers, who are sometimes called the Magisterial Reformers, but they were not alone in breaking from the Roman Catholic Church in the sixteenth century. There is a large and rather disparate group of Christians who are sometimes called Anabaptists, but perhaps better termed part of the Radical Reformation. Many were marked by their rejection of infant baptism and their hesitation to pledge allegiance to the state. While some in this group, including Menno Simons (1496–1561), affirmed traditional understandings of hell, others did not. Simons spoke of his desire to point persons to Christ, for it would be

> unmerciful to tyrannically offer this poor soul which was purchased with such precious treasure to the devil of hell, under the unbearable judgment, punishment, and wrath of God, so that he would forever have to suffer and bear the tortures of the unquenchable burning, the consuming fire, eternal pain, woe, and death. Never taking into consideration the Son of man who says, "Learn of me, I have given you an example, follow me, I am not come to destroy souls but to save them."[7]

What marked most so-called Anabaptists was a rejection of the Reformed/Lutheran view of election. They believed that Christ died for all persons, making it possible for all to come to faith. Some moved in a universalist direction, or at least, like Hans Denck (c. 1495–1527), a south German Anabaptist of the sixteenth century, were accused of universalism. Denck insisted that Christ died for all, allowing for the possibility of all being saved, though not everyone would choose salvation. Elements of his writings, even if not explicit, gave opponents cause to believe that he leaned toward universalism, including parallels to Origen.[8] There was a strong interest in Christ's descent into Hades, such that he redeemed the Old Testament saints as well as some good pagans. For some, such as Pilgrim Marpeck (d. 1556), this descent into Hades was a literal event that involved Christ preaching a gospel of forgiveness in hell. What marked many Anabaptists was a rejection of predestination as understood by Luther and Calvin. They believed in free will, the idea that a person is free to choose either heaven or hell by choosing to believe (or not believe) in Christ.

Before moving into the future, we need to acknowledge the Roman Catholic counterpoint. Regarding the doctrine of hell itself, there is little difference with the Reformers. As to purgatory, there is a major difference. Luther, due in part to his protest against the abuses relating to the selling of indulgences, raised concerns about purgatory, not the least being that he found no scriptural support for the doctrine. Zwingli was more specific in his rejection of purgatory, calling purgatory as taught by Roman Catholics a "figment of their own invention."[9] The Catholic response was laid out in a decree of the Council of Trent in 1547. Drawing on their reading of Scripture and tradition, the council taught that not only did purgatory exist but "the souls detained there are helped by the prayers of the faithful, and especially by the acceptable Sacrifice of the Altar."[10]

In the aftermath of the Reformation, Roman Catholics responded with the Council of Trent as well as new religious orders, the most important being the Jesuits. As Alice Turner notes, the view of hell changed with the Jesuits. "Horrid as the old Hell was, it had variety, activity, scenery, and a certain entertainment value—too much, in fact, for the Jesuits. It might frighten the uneducated into good behavior, but it was not taken seriously by the people who counted. So, the Jesuits dispensed with the frills." While they eliminated much of the torture and the monsters, "what they added was unnervingly apt for the times—they added urban squalor."[11]

With that in mind, we turn to what Jesuit founder Ignatius of Loyola wrote about hell in the fifth exercise of his *Spiritual Exercises*. In this "Meditation on Hell," Ignatius invites those participating in the exercise, after their preparatory prayer, to use their imagination to envision the "length, breadth, and depth of hell." This involves gaining an "interior sense of the pain suffered by the damned, so that if through my faults I should forget the love of the Eternal Lord, at least the fear of those pains will serve to keep me from falling into sin." From there he meditates on the nature of the experiences of those consigned to hell and why they are there. With that, he gives thanks to Christ because Christ has not let him fall into the classes of those consigned to hell. Thus, in many ways, he is like the Protestant Reformers in that he sees the possibility of hell being a warning to remain faithful to Christ.[12]

Post-Reformation Developments

Moving into the post-Reformation period, on the Protestant side of things, we see a tightening up of the thought of the Reformers. At the same time, with the advent of the Enlightenment at the end of the seventeenth century, more questions begin to be raised about the reasonableness of hell. Additionally, questions are raised about the mortality of the soul. This latter question emerges in a variety of places, including the earlier Radical Reformation. Among others reframing the idea of eternal punishment, we can count philosopher Thomas Hobbes (1588–1679).

For Hobbes, the idea of natural immortality is rooted in Greek thinking and not biblical thought. Philip Almond notes that for Hobbes, who was theologically unorthodox, "immortality was not the soul's natural right to an existence outside of time, but was a supernatural gift conferred upon the bodies of the elect in a future time." While agreeing that the wicked would face judgment, he interpreted the idea of the fire of judgment in terms of annihilation, not eternal torment.[13]

The more orthodox John Milton (1608–74) also rejected natural immortality, doing so based on Scripture. Like Hobbes, he believed in postresurrection immortality, with the righteous being rewarded and the wicked punished. However, Milton did not follow Hobbes regarding the annihilation of the soul. Milton's understanding of the afterlife is found in his epic poem *Paradise Lost*. For Milton, hell is ready to receive inhabitants, but contrary to Calvin's vision of hell being a matter of predestination, no one is foreordained to enter hell.

Another important Puritan figure of the seventeenth century was John Bunyan (1628–88), best known for his *Pilgrim's Progress*. Bunyan took a traditional view of hell, including envisioning the damned experiencing the flames of hell. Perhaps this description of the state of those condemned offers another dimension, emphasizing the eternal experience of a guilty conscience:

> As the Just shall arise as spiritual Bodies, so the unjust shall arise only as mere and naked lumps of sinful nature, not having the least help from God to bear them up under this condition, Wherefore, so soon as ever they are risen out of their Graves, they will feel a continual sinking under every remembrance of every sin and thoughts of Judgment; in their rising they fall, fall I say from thenceforth, and forever. And for this Reason, the Dungeon into which they fall is called *bottomless*. Because, as there will be no end of their misery, so there will be no stay or prop to bear them up in it.[14]

Still in the seventeenth century, while some had questions about hell, the primary purpose of hell was as a deterrent to sin, though the idea of vindictive justice remained part of orthodox Catholic and Protestant understandings of hell. There was, to be sure, some desire to mitigate the nature of hell, but even most advocates of abolishing eternal torment wished to keep some duration of torment as a deterrent against sin.

One area of movement even among Protestants who insisted on the eternal nature of hell's torments was questions about the damnation of infants, a doctrine that Augustine embraced due to his view of original sin. While Catholics had the option of limbo, which was a place of separation but not torment, Protestants, for the most part, did not. Thus, many began abandoning the idea of infant damnation as one form of mitigation of hell.

Age of Enlightenment

By the late seventeenth century, the Enlightenment had begun to take hold. With it came a call for a more reasonable form of Christianity. Thus, when it came to mitigating the torment of hell for those other than infants, some began to question the eternity of hell, including leading theologians and philosophers of the English Enlightenment such as John Locke, Isaac Newton, William Whiston, and Samuel Clarke.

John Tillotson, archbishop of Canterbury, preached the sermon "Of the Eternity of Hell-Torments" before Queen Mary II and King William III in 1696 and revealed interesting possibilities when it comes to mitigation. Drawing from Matthew 25:46, he assumes that on the day of judgment, the just will go to heaven for eternity and the damned to hell, but he offers a caveat. He acknowledges that some have called into question the justice of persons suffering eternal torment for temporary sins. Nevertheless, there is concern for the deterrent effect of the fear of hell that needs to be maintained. So, he is very clear that no one should assume that God will not act in judgment; such judgment is torment, not annihilation, which he does not believe is a sufficient deterrent. Having said all that, he makes a distinction between threats and the execution of those threats:

> He that threatens keeps the right of punishing in his own hand and is not obliged to execute what he hath threatened any further than the reasons and ends of Government do require. And he may without any injury to the party threatened remit and abate as much as he pleaseth of the punishment that he hath threatened and because in so doing he is not worse but better than his word nobody can find fault or complain of any wrong or injustice thereby done to him.[15]

As Philip Almond points out, for Tillotson, God might offer hope of salvation beyond the grave, but it is "prudent to continue to act as if the doctrine of eternal punishments were true." As Almond notes, with that caveat about God doing what God pleases when it comes to carrying out a threat, Tillotson extends "to divine justice a principle which had become fundamental in English criminal law by the late seventeenth century, and common after the development of transportation in 1718, that of royal pardon from capital punishments."[16] (Transportation in this sense involved exiling convicted but pardoned criminals first to Jamaica and then to Australia.)

As we enter the eighteenth century, with the Age of Enlightenment and its emphasis on the role of reason, a perspective that led to questioning received church traditions was in full bloom. Nevertheless, there remained little sympathy for the mitigation of the threat of hell. We see the full embrace of the doctrine of hell in the theology of Jonathan Edwards, who was well versed in Enlightenment thinking, following John Calvin's lead regarding divine judgment and the eternal nature of hell, a view expressed in his famed sermon "Sinners in the Hands of an Angry God," with more ferocity. Unlike Tillotson, Edwards believed that God carried out God's threats. Edwards (1703–58) was a leading American Puritan theologian and minister who believed that hell was an imminent threat to the unconverted, and therefore it should be utilized with ferocity, to warn both the sheep and the unconverted. In his sermon he emphasized that God has the power to throw the wicked into hell and no one has the power to resist God. This is simply a matter of divine justice, for the wicked deserve their fate. Thus, the "wrath of God burns against them, their damnation does not slumber; the pit is prepared, the fire is made ready, the furnace is now hot, ready to receive them; the flames do now rage and glow."[17] One should not assume that this is not one's fate.

In contrast to Edwards's Calvinist embrace of the message of hell, with its dependence on Calvin's view of double predestination, such that some were consigned to heaven and some to hell through an eternal decree from before time, stands John Wesley (1703–91). Wesley rejected the Calvinist understanding of predestination. On one hand, Wesley, like Edwards, believed that after the day of judgment, the wicked would suffer eternal punishment in hell along with the devil and his angels. We see how he developed his understanding of hell in two sermons. First, in his "Great Assize" sermon from 1758, which drew upon Romans 14:10, he connects the eternal nature of the punishment of the wicked to the eternal nature of the reward given to the righteous. Unlike Tillotson, Wesley could not envision separating the two judgments. The eternity of heaven was linked to the eternity of punishment in hell.[18] Wesley used his sermon "Of Hell" to speak of the horrors of eternal banishment from the presence of God and the fiery torment experienced by those sentenced to hell. Banishment was for Wesley the equivalent of "eternal destruction," and the fires of hell were not metaphorical. He addressed those who suggested that references to the wicked being cast into the lake of fire led to annihilation by following Augustine and insisting that the resurrection body, which both the righteous and the wicked receive at the general resurrection, is capable of being cast into the fire and not consumed. Therefore, the torment experienced by those cast into hell is eternal.[19]

On the other hand, Wesley disagreed with Edwards due to Wesley's embrace of free will, such that when it comes to following Christ and receiving God's grace on the day of judgment, each person has a choice between heaven and hell. That message is revealed in his sermon "On Eternity": "I say, made choice; for it is impossible this should be the lot of any creature but by his own act and deed. The day is coming when every soul will be constrained to acknowledge, in the sight of men and angels, no dire decree of thine did seal or fix the unalterable doom, consign my unborn soul to hell, or damn me from my mother's womb."[20] For Wesley, humans must be free to make their own choices, even if God foreknows those choices; otherwise, they cannot be held accountable for their decisions and actions.

While the majority position throughout the period from the Reformation through the eighteenth century insisted that hell was the destiny of the wicked, such that Edwards and Wesley were on the same page, there were pockets of resistance. At least some people questioned the doctrine of hell and held out the possibility of universal salvation. Among them were the Pietist Johann

Wilhelm Petersen (1649–1726) and the Moravian leader Nicholas von Zinzendorf (1700–1760). In England, a group of millennialist mystics known as the Philadelphians, a name taken from the church of Philadelphia in the book of Revelation, gathered around Jane Lead, known for her visions, in the late seventeenth century and embraced universal restoration. In addition, the Anglican spiritual writer William Law (1686–1761) appears to have embraced a form of universalism, at least later in life after encountering the work of the mystic Jacob Böhme. In his work *The Spirit of Prayer*, Law envisions hell as something internal to the human being, something that Christ drives out of us because of his death on the cross, though he does not see the cross as atoning God's wrath:

> God has so loved the world, that his only Son hung and expired, bleeding on the cross, not to atone his own wrath against us, but to extinguish our own hell within us, to pour his heavenly love into us, to show us that meekness, suffering, and dying to our own fallen nature, is the one, only possible way, for fallen man to be alive again in God.[21]

Nineteenth-Century Perspectives

As we enter the nineteenth century, the majority position remains in place. The wicked face the prospect of eternity in hell. That may be their eternal destiny due to God's predetermination or the choice to not follow Christ. Samuel Taylor Coleridge was clear in his belief that "punishment is essentially vindictive, i.e. expressive of abhorrence of sin for its own exceeding sinfulness: from all experience as well as *a priori* from the constitution of the human Soul I gather that without a miraculous intervention of Omnipotence the Punishment must continue as long as the Soul, which I believe, imperishable." He did not believe that God would provide such a miracle.[22]

One nineteenth-century preacher who continued to emphasize God's justice and the promise of divine wrath and eternal torment for the wicked was Charles Haddon Spurgeon (1834–92), the famous British preacher and evangelist. He affirmed God's love and mercy, but he also emphasized God's justice, which meant the damnation of the wicked. It also meant that a faithful preacher should make this known. In his sermon "Turn or Burn," preached in 1856, Spurgeon declared:

> They preach of God's love and mercy as they ought to do, and as God has commanded them; but of what avail is it to preach mercy unless they preach also the doom of the wicked? And how shall we hope to effect the purpose of preaching unless we warn men that if they "turn not, he will whet his sword?" I fear that in too many places the doctrine of future punishment is rejected and laughed as a fancy and a chimera; but the day will come when it shall be known to be a reality.[23]

In a sermon from 1862, Spurgeon makes it clear that punishment in hell is horrific and eternal:

> Here we have a pause in our pain; the fever has its rests; paroxysms of agony have their seasons of quiet; but there in hell the gnashing of teeth shall be unceasing, the worm's gnawings shall know no cessation; on, on forever—forever a hot race of misery. Then, worst of all, it shall be without end. When ten thousand years have run their course, thou shalt be no nearer to the end than at first.[24]

Spurgeon saw it as his duty, as his act of love, to make this message clear.

While the nineteenth century would see a decline in emphasis on hell, as Spurgeon himself noted, still many Christians continued to view hell as an essential component of traditional Christianity. We see this in the teachings of Anglican theologian and later Roman Catholic Cardinal John Henry Newman, who fully embraced the doctrine of eternal punishment. It was a view he inherited from his Calvinist evangelical origins, but which he also believed was delivered by Jesus. He wrote in his *Apologia pro Vita Sua:* "From this time I have held with a full inward assent and belief the doctrine of eternal punishment, as delivered by our Lord Himself, in as true a sense as I hold that of eternal happiness; though I have tried in various ways to make that truth less terrible to the imagination."[25] Those who continued to embrace the idea of hell as a place of eternal torment were often concerned about holiness and recognizing the severity of sin and its consequences.

Most Christians during the nineteenth century continued to embrace the doctrine of eternal torment, as Spurgeon and others presented it; nevertheless, others took different paths. Some were liberals, but not all. Some affirmed universalism and others conditionalism or annihilationism. Many who embrace these alternatives root their beliefs theologically in the love of God and pastorally because traditional teachings on hell cause psychological trauma. Nevertheless, the majority position, at least at the level of formal church doctrine and in much popular piety, remains the belief that the wicked or those who do not confess Christ as savior will experience eternal punishment in hell.

Universalism is the idea that everyone will be saved. Among the earliest proponents of true universalism was James Relly (1720–78), who began preaching a universalist message in England that led to the conversion of the Calvinist John Murray (1741–1815), who moved from England to New Jersey in 1770 and began preaching universal salvation in the colonies. Murray had originally been a follower of George Whitefield but had a change of heart while reading Relly's works. He became a well-known and popular exponent of universalism. Another figure in this move toward universalism in the United States was Elhanan Winchester (1751–97), who formed the Universal Baptist Church in 1781. By 1790 a Universalist Convocation met that became the foundation of the Universalist Church. These early universalists were orthodox in their theology, except concerning eternal torment. While they might believe in the existence of hell, they believed it was temporary and corrective. In time this universalist movement would embrace Unitarianism, largely due to the embrace of rationalism by universalist leaders such as Hosea Ballou (1771–1852). As for Unitarians, most continued to believe in an afterlife and might see the possibility of postmortem punishment, but instead of it being vindictive they understood it to be reformatory.[26] Unitarian writer Lant Carpenter insisted that retributive punishment did not accord with God's intentions. Thus, "when suffering has done its work, and the deep stains of guilt have been removed as by fire, suffering will be no longer continued."[27]

The decline in adherence to belief in hell in the nineteenth century was influenced in part by the implications of Darwin's theory of evolution for theology. Both universalism and the idea of eternal punishment rested on a belief in an immortal soul. Darwin's theories raised questions about an immortal soul, which led a growing number of people to embrace the idea of conditional immortality. As Geoffrey Rowell notes, conditional immortality "emerged as one of the attempts to find a mediating position between the extremes of universalism and eternal punishment, and, in particular, it was influenced by a revulsion from the cruder forms of missionary theology."[28] Conditionalists taught that humans were created mortal but with the capacity for immortality, which, at least among most Christian adherents, depended on faith in Christ. Conditionalists might teach that annihilation took place at death or later after the wicked had been punished. Conditionalism appealed to different parts of the Christian community, including proponents of Christian missionary efforts. While the threat of hell had been used as a foundation for missionary efforts, some began to question the justness of condemning the vast number of persons who had yet to hear the gospel. Thus, as Rowell points out, "Conditionalism with its warning of the annihilation of the wicked, seemed to be in a position to restore the note of urgency to missionary work, whilst avoiding the harshness of supposing that God had condemned large numbers of men to eternal torment."[29]

Conditionalism originally emerged largely within Reformed and Calvinist communities as a mitigation of the harshness of an Augustinian understanding of hell. Many turned to Irenaeus's view of immortality being a gift of God for patristic support. As Rowell writes, "Those conditionalists who drew on contemporary evolutionary theory, however, did approach much more closely to the Irenaean view, and emphasized the possibilities of growth and development open to man in a way which is reminiscent of what [John] Hick has called the 'vale of soul-making' theodicy."[30]

While neither universalism nor conditionalism completely replaced belief in hell, hell was largely ignored as the nineteenth century progressed. As Gary Scott Smith notes, "After 1870 few revivalists used 'terror tactics.' Gilded Age evangelists typically highlighted the blessedness of heaven much more than the dreadfulness of hell to goad the ungodly to repent." We see this in the decision made by evangelist Dwight L. Moody, who, according to Smith, "concluded that he could win more converts by accentuating the love of God and the wonders of heaven than by using images of hellfire and damnation to frighten his auditors."[31]

In bringing this chapter to a close, we look at the father of modern theology, Friedrich Schleiermacher (1768–1834), whose theological work proved influential. Schleiermacher's move toward universal salvation and restoration of all things began as he reexamined the Reformed doctrine of election, including predestination. In Schleiermacher's view, the problem was not election. It was damnation. Thus, he called for a full embrace of God's decree of election but minus the doctrine of hell.[32] To understand Schleiermacher's theology, we must first take note of the connection he made between a "feeling of absolute dependence" and being in relationship to God. As for redemption and election, Schleiermacher took a cautious approach. While affirming, to a point, an Augustinian/Calvinist understanding of predestination, he advocated for one form of predestination rather than two, with some redeemed and elected and the others damned. In proposition 119 of his *Christian Faith,* he writes: "Suppose that instead we proceed based on the presupposition that all who belong to the human race would, sometime or other, be taken up into community of life with Christ."[33] In a postscript on eternal damnation Schleiermacher writes: "If we now consider eternal damnation in its relation to eternal blessedness, it is easy to see that if eternal damnation exists, eternal blessedness cannot continue to exist."[34] In making this point he is clear that one cannot experience eternal blessedness while knowing that others are experiencing torment. Regarding eternal damnation, Schleiermacher concludes:

> Thus, viewed from both sides, there are great difficulties in trying to envisage that the eventual outcome of redemption would be such that thereby some would have a share in supreme blessedness but others—and indeed according to the conventional notion the largest portion of the human race—would be irretrievably lost in a state lacking blessedness. In consequence, we should not cling to such a notion without decisive evidence that Christ himself foresaw this outcome in that fashion, and in no way do we have such evidence. Hence, we surely ought, at the

very least, to grant equal right to that more moderate outlook of which there are also still some traces in Scripture, namely that by the power of redemption a general restoration of all human souls would eventually occur.[35]

Throughout the nineteenth century, we see the beginnings of major questions being raised regarding hell and eternal damnation. Many Christian denominations would continue to hold to traditional views of eternal damnation moving into the twentieth century. Others would embrace conditionalism as a middle path between eternal damnation and universalism. Still others would follow people like Schleiermacher and question the viability of the doctrine and move toward various forms of universalism. Whichever path we choose to embrace, it is worth considering this word from Geoffrey Rowell:

> We cannot do without a doctrine of hell, for it stands as a vitally important reminder of the reality and seriousness of the experience of alienation, isolation, and estrangement, and the consequences of evil in human life, though to speak of hell can so easily make God morally obnoxious and repellent. In eschatology, as in other areas of theology, the theologian's path is perilous, as the men of the nineteenth century, who debated the issues with such agony and passion knew to their cost. The least we can say of them is that in their controversies they not only uncovered the confusions of the past, but they also opened up perspectives of vital importance for the future.[36]

To that future, we now turn.

Part 3

Voices Nuancing the Discussion about Hell

In part 3 we consider voices that articulate distinctive perspectives on hell, some from the late nineteenth century and many from the twentieth. Chapter 6 focuses on the Roman Catholic traditions. With chapter 7, we begin a series of explorations of voices that came to expression in the twentieth century: voices that seek to "modernize" hell, especially Rudolf Bultmann and Paul Tillich (chap. 7); figurative pictures of hell in Karl Barth and the postliberals (chap. 8); three apocalyptic theologians—Ernst Käsemann, Jürgen Moltmann, and Wolfhart Pannenberg (chap. 9); and the perspectives of liberation theology (chap. 10) and open and relational (including process) theologies (chap. 11).

Chapter 6

Voices from the Roman Catholic Church

*M*odern Roman Catholic teaching around punishment includes four main foci: hell, eternal damnation, purgatory, and final judgment. Roman Catholic teaching today has its roots in interpretations of Scripture, as well as the writings of Augustine and Thomas Aquinas. Augustine, as we have seen in chapter 5, set the course of Western or Latin Christianity that continues with modification and development into the present. For Augustine, because of the fall, God deemed all of humanity guilty of original sin and thus condemnation. However, God has chosen some for salvation, while all others are condemned to eternal damnation. Thomas Aquinas followed Augustine, providing more definition of the nature of hell; like Augustine, he said that those not chosen are condemned to suffer eternal torment. When it comes to modern understandings, because Vatican II did not address this question, we must start with Vatican I (1869–70).

The decree of Vatican I that deals with the final judgment declares that there is no room for repentance after death. Therefore, those "who die in actual mortal sin are excluded from the kingdom of God and will suffer forever the torments of hell where there is no redemption. Also, those who die with only original sin will never have the holy vision of God."[1] Purgatory, which is understood to be an intermediate stage between death and one's final state (heaven), is not seen as a place of redemption for those not already redeemed. Instead, it is a place of purification and transformation for those who died before fulfilling their penance. As to the nature of purgatory, Elmar Klinger writes that "the decisive documents do not impose any obligation as regards fire, a place of purification, or the duration, kind and intrinsic nature of punishment."[2]

Regarding the doctrine of hell itself, according to the official Catechism of the Catholic Church, "The teaching of the Church affirms the existence of hell and its eternity. Immediately after death, the souls of those who die in a state of mortal sin descend into hell, where they suffer the punishments of hell, 'eternal fire.' The chief punishment of hell is eternal separation from God, in whom alone man can possess the life and happiness for which he was created and for which he longs."[3] The catechism also makes it clear that God does not predestine anyone to hell, but those who are condemned to hell go to hell because of their willful persistence in rejecting God's mercy. While this is the church's official teaching, when asked in an interview about his view of hell, Pope Francis stated, "What I would say is not a dogma of faith, but my personal thought: I like to think hell is empty; I hope it is."[4] Francis's hopeful view of hell's emptiness may stem from his embrace of God's merciful nature. In a book published early in his papacy, at the time that Francis declared a Jubilee Year of Mercy, he offered that "the Church condemns sin because it has to relay the truth: 'This is a sin.' But at the same time, it embraces the sinner who recognizes himself as such, it welcomes him, it speaks to him of the infinite mercy of God."[5] While Francis does not speak of hell in this book, he emphasizes God's mercy and desire to forgive all who would embrace God's love.

With this conciliar statement and the church's catechism as a starting point, we will look at several more recent theological discussions of hell, including those of Joseph Ratzinger (Pope Benedict XVI from 2005 to 2013), Karl Rahner, Hans Urs von Balthasar, and Hans Küng, who were all leading and influential Catholic theologians. We begin with Ratzinger's brief discussion of hell in his book *Eschatology: Death and Eternal Life,* the second edition published in 1988, before his election to the papacy. In the discussion that follows, when we speak about the contributions of Father Ratzinger—to become Pope Benedict—we will distinguish between Benedict XVI's papal statements and his earlier writings by using the appropriate name.

Joseph Ratzinger (Pope Benedict XVI)

Ratzinger (1927–2022) begins his discussion of hell by noting that "the idea of eternal damnation, which had taken ever clearer shape in the Judaism of the century or two before Christ, has a firm place in the teaching of Jesus, as well as the apostolic writings." Therefore, the church's dogma stands on solid ground when it comes to its teachings on hell's existence and the eternity of its punishments.[6] Ratzinger notes the difficulties posed by the doctrine, pointing to the responses of Origen, Gregory of Nyssa, and others, but when it comes to the mainstream of church teaching, it must be acknowledged that the idea of universal reconciliation does not reflect the biblical witness. Therefore, according to Ratzinger, one must acknowledge "God's unconditional respect for the freedom of his creature," such that they might receive God's love, but humanity has the freedom to resist. Therefore, humans have the final responsibility for their destiny: "Heaven reposes upon freedom, and so leaves to the damned the right to will their own damnation."[7]

He acknowledges the existence of an intermediate state between death and final judgment, which in the Latin church came to be known as purgatory. Purgatory served as a place of purification. As with the doctrine of hell, Ratzinger roots the concept of purgatory in ancient Judaism, especially 2 Maccabees, where prayers were offered that the sin of those who apostatized would be blotted out. For Ratzinger, purgatory is rooted in the practice of penance. It is, he writes, "the inwardly necessary process of transformation in which a person becomes capable of Christ, capable of God and thus capable of unity with the whole communion of saints. . . . It does not replace grace by works, but allows the former to achieve its full victory precisely as grace. What actually saves is the full assent of faith. But in most of us, that basic option is buried under a great deal of wood, hay, and straw." Therefore, the experience of purgatory, which is part of the intermediate state, is an expression of divine mercy, but that mercy "does not exonerate him from the need to be transformed."[8] Ratzinger represents the traditional Roman Catholic position, but, as do other leading Catholic theologians, he offers that doctrine with nuance.

In his definitive statements in his book *Eschatology*, he devotes less space to describing hell than to purgatory.

Karl Rahner

Karl Rahner (1904–84), who is considered one of the leading twentieth-century Roman Catholic theologians and a key figure at the Second Vatican Council, affirms the church's teaching concerning the existence of hell as well as its eternity. However, he offers significant nuances to this doctrine, noting that the church has not produced official declarations concerning the nature of the punishments in hell. With that in mind, Rahner emphasizes human freedom to say no to God, which incurs "eternal loss." This no to God ultimately is rooted in the mystery of evil that takes hold of a person. Rahner writes that this "possibility of a 'no' to God himself can become a reality in [a person] in the sense that in his subjectivity, which he cannot distinguish from himself and shirk responsibility for, he really is evil, and he understands this evil as what he is and what he definitively wants to be."[9] While Rahner acknowledges the church's teaching on hell, he also suggests that "speculations about the 'place' where hell is to be found are pointless. There is no possibility of inserting hell into the empirical world around us."[10] For Rahner, to speak of hell is to speak of "eternal loss" in the sense of separation from God. As for the details of the next life, including the severity and extent of the pains suffered, that is beyond the capacity of theology to determine. What the church is called to do then is "maintain side by side and unwaveringly the truth of the omnipotence of the universal salvific will of God, the redemption of all by Christ, the duty of all men to hope for salvation and also the true possibility of eternal loss."[11]

Saying no to God has self-destructive consequences. As for the idea of hell more specifically, Rahner speaks in terms of "eternal loss." He does not focus on the content of hell, but when it comes to Jesus' statements about the "last judgment and its outcome," we need not read anything into it "but that a person has to reckon with the possibility of eternal loss."[12] The preacher is called to hold out the "possibility of hell as perpetual obduracy" while also offering "insistent encouragement to rely with confidence on the infinite mercy of God."[13] Rahner seeks to balance human freedom to say no to God while holding out the reality of God's mercy. As for God's part in the punishments experienced in hell, God is not the one who inflicts them. However, God does not release those in hell from the "state which man himself has achieved on his own behalf, contradictory though this state be to the world as God's creation."[14] Rahner may affirm the church's teachings, but he offers no description of the nature of punishment and insists that humanity has the freedom to say yes or no to God's mercy. Without embracing the doctrine of *apokatastasis,* he holds out the hope of the redemption of all humanity.

Hans Urs von Balthasar

Hans Urs von Balthasar (1905–88), a Swiss theologian, wrote about hell in a provocatively titled book, *Dare We Hope: "That All Men Be Saved"?* The book's critics charged him with universalism, a charge he rejected. Balthasar used Scripture and tradition to demonstrate that it would be just for God to allow humans to suffer the eternal consequences of sin; however, it is within God's mercy to commute that sentence. Therefore, "insofar as God bestows upon creatures what they deserve, he is just; insofar as he bestows it upon them not for the sake of his own advantage but purely out of goodness and insofar as the perfections bestowed upon things by God overcome anything defective, he acts mercifully."[15] Pope Francis pondered the possibility that while hell exists, it might be empty; Balthasar raises a similar possibility. He starts with the premise that all humanity lies under judgment and therefore will face God's judgment seat, but he offers God's mercy as a response. Like Rahner, he rejected the doctrine of *apokatastasis* (the restoration of all things). In his *Short Discourse on Hell,* which was a response to the original edition of *Dare We Hope,* von Balthasar insists that hell is a real possibility, but he does not follow Augustine in asserting that hell is an "objective certainty."

He offers as his solution the premise that "God does not damn anyone, but that the man who irrevocably refuses love condemns himself."[16] The question that he raises is whether the one who refuses God's love will hold firm to the end. Some say yes, that some will refuse God's love to the very end. Von Balthasar calls these persons "infernalists." A second group, among whom he identifies himself, does not know whether those who at first resist will at some point respond positively, and therefore it is possible to hold out hope "that the light of divine love will ultimately be able to penetrate every human darkness and refusal."[17] While he acknowledges the presence of scriptural texts that threaten divine punishment, he also acknowledges the presence of universalist passages. With this in mind, he claims that it is possible to hold out hope for the salvation of all people without rejecting the possibility that hell might not be empty. Thus, he refrains from embracing universalism. As he writes, "Faith in the unboundedness of divine love and grace also justifies *hope for the universality of redemption,* although, through the possibility of resistance to grace that remains open in principle, the *possibility* of eternal damnation also persists." The key here is the premise that human freedom cannot be overridden by divine freedom. Nevertheless, when it comes to divine love "there are *no limits* to how far it may extend."[18] Therefore, we are under obligation to hope for the salvation and redemption of all persons.

Hans Küng

Hans Küng (1928–2021), the longtime professor of theology at Tübingen University, was stripped of his position as a Roman Catholic theologian in the 1980s; however, he represents a progressive Catholic theological perspective. In his book *Eternal Life?*, Küng writes that while the earliest creeds say little about hell, over time it became a central teaching of the church. Therefore, it cannot be dismissed in silence because "it has done immense harm over the course of centuries." Teachings on hell created fear and led to all manner of persecutions, often in pursuit of redemption of unbelievers and heretics. To overcome this history, one must uncover its origins and critically examine the doctrine.[19] In doing this work of critical reflection, Küng looks to Jesus, who he notes spoke of hell using apocalyptic language. Nevertheless, Jesus was not a hellfire preacher and sought to free people from demons. Küng rejects the dualism of God and devil, heaven and hell, as if one requires the other. That does not mean evil does not exist, but the question is what this says about hell and its eternal nature. At least since the sixth century the majority position within the Christian community, Catholic, Orthodox, and Protestant, is that the punishment of hell lasts forever; it is eternal. That view, however, runs counter to the mercy and love of God. As for the idea that it is not God who damns, but that human beings due to inherent freedom choose to damn themselves, that perspective is also questionable.

However, recognizing that humans are not completely good or completely bad, they still must die into God, which he believes has a "judicial-purifying character." He rejects the mythological view of hell as a place in the underworld but rather sees it as a theological matter that speaks of "an exclusion from the fellowship of the living God, described in a variety of images but nevertheless unimaginable, as the absolutely final possibility of distance from God, which man cannot *a priori* exclude." Thus, it is important to take seriously the possibility of eternal failure but also find hope in the promises in the New Testament of God's universal mercy. "The eternity of the 'punishment of hell' (of the 'fire'), asserted in some New Testament metaphorical expressions, remains subject to God and to his will. Individual New Testament texts, which are not balanced by others, suggest the consummation of a salvation of all, an all-embracing mercy."[20] For Hans Küng, hell cannot have the last word.

We have looked at four figures who represent the perspective of the Roman Catholic Church in the twentieth and twenty-first centuries. None of them represent all Catholics, but they do provide a breadth of perspective. While the majority position within the church still asserts the existence of hell, there is hope offered that hell might be empty. The onus is not put on God, who, according to these theologians, does not condemn to hell. The question then is whether it is possible that in God's mercy hell is indeed empty.

As Hans Urs von Balthasar asks: "Dare we hope?" Pope Francis, for his part, would seem to answer yes to von Balthasar's question; he puts his hope in the mercy of God.

Chapter 7

Voices from the Modern Worldview

Bultmann and Tillich

We turn now to attempts on the part of thinkers to "modernize hell," that is, to describe the experience of hell in modern terms. This chapter focuses on two well-known figures from an earlier era, Rudolf Bultmann (1884–1986) and Paul Tillich (1886–1965). Their approaches are similar enough to discuss them under the general idea of modernizing hell, but they are different enough to deserve separate comment.

To understand their approaches, we must understand the differences between the pre-Enlightenment (or premodern) worldview and the Enlightenment (or modern) worldview. The attempts to modernize views of hell seek to leave pre-Enlightenment (premodern) perspectives behind and replace them with Enlightenment (modern) points of view. For the purposes of this discussion (and for getting inside many theological conversations), it is important to note that here "modern" means not just contemporary or up-to-date (as in "our house has a modern kitchen") but consistent with Enlightenment perspectives. Modern theology, for instance, is theology that is expressed in terms of the modern (Enlightenment) point of view.

Pre-Enlightenment (Premodern) Thinking

The story of the efforts to modernize hell begins with the background of how many people understood the world before the Enlightenment (which began in the late 1600s). In the pre-Enlightenment age, many people assumed that tradition was the primary source of authority. If God, the Bible, the teaching of the church, or other authoritative voices from the past said something, pre-Enlightenment people tended to believe those sources. From their point of view, authoritative voices from tradition speak truth. A good many people assumed that God could directly intervene in the world to bring about help or harm and that supernatural beings inhabited and affected the world.

Many pre-Enlightenment communities used mythological language to set out their interpretations of the world. Scholars remind us that in this context a myth is not merely a statement that is not true. Rather, for pre-Enlightenment communities, a myth is a story involving characters (especially deities) and actions that explain the way things are. Communities tell myths to interpret such things as the origins of the world, where human beings came from, the purposes of human life, and the relationship between humankind and nature. For example, the Babylonians told a myth about the creation of the world that involved a fight between two deities. One divine being killed the other and fashioned the world out of the body of the dead deity. The idea that the world was created through violence (the fight between the deities) authorized the practice of violence in the world.

Enlightenment (Modern) Thinking

As we said earlier, the Enlightenment began in the late 1600s and eventually held sway over many communities until the late twentieth century, when postmodernity began to question some Enlightenment (or modern) perspectives. For our discussion, the most important aspects of modernity are sources of authority, the scientific worldview, and the different functions of language. Enlightenment thinkers regarded previous methods of thinking as dim and only partially reliable. The Enlightenment turned up the lights of science and reason.

One key to the modern mind-set is the scientific worldview, which seeks to describe the world objectively. Modern people accept as trustworthy and truthful those things that can be verified by science. Modern people also trust what is considered reasonable and can be confirmed by empirical observation. When it comes to the language used to describe the world, modern thinkers seek precision.

Based on this modern worldview, mythological language cannot be deemed trustworthy because it is not consistent with scientific descriptions of the way the world operates. While modern thinkers might appreciate the use of metaphor, story, poetry, and similar modes of language to express human feelings about the world, that is not the same thing as describing the world in scientific terms.

Rudolf Bultmann and Demythologizing

Rudolf Bultmann, a Lutheran, followed by many New Testament scholars, viewed the "world picture of the New Testament" as being "mythical" in nature. New Testament writers believed that "the world is a three-story structure, with earth in the middle, heaven above it, and hell below it." In this construction of the world, "heaven is the dwelling place of God and of heavenly figures—the angels; the world below is hell, the place of torment. But even the earth is not simply the scene of natural, day-to-day occurrences . . . It is a theater for the working of supernatural powers, God and his angels, Satan and his demons on the other."[1]

Bultmann says such mythological talk is "incredible to men and women today because for them the mythical world picture is a thing of the past."[2] When Bultmann says mythological talk is obsolete, he means it is not believable. Bultmann assumes that contemporary women and men do not think mythologically. This raises the question of what—if anything—people today can make of a faith that was originally communicated in a mythical form. What sense does it make to speak of hell as a place of torment when we no longer believe the universe is comprised of three stories?

Bultmann answers these questions by pointing to the process of demythologizing. The word "demythologizing" could be taken to imply getting rid of myth. While that element is present, Bultmann means something more. The "aim is not to eliminate the mythological elements but to interpret them."[3] The myth is like the husk on an ear of corn. It serves as a cultural wrapping, such that when the husk (myth) is pulled off, a core of meaning (similar to the actual ear of corn) remains. The myth is the surface meaning but there is a deeper meaning, a significance, that goes beyond the myth. For Bultmann, mythic expression points to experience in the world, leading him to seek to translate mythological language into concepts that are at home in modernity. For example, "According to mythological thinking, God has [God's] domicile in heaven. What is the meaning of this statement? The meaning is quite clear. In a crude manner it expresses the idea that God is beyond the world, that [God] is transcendent."[4]

Bultmann applies this approach to hell:

> When mythological thinking forms the conception of hell, it expresses the idea of the transcendence of evil as the tremendous power which again and again afflicts mankind. The location of hell and of [people] whom hell has seized is below the earth in darkness, because darkness is tremendous and terrible to [people].
>
> These mythological conceptions of heaven and hell are no longer acceptable for modern [people] since for scientific thinking to speak of "above" and "below" in the universe has lost all meaning, but the idea of the transcendence of God and of evil is still significant.[5]

For Bultmann, the call of God comes to each person in every moment to pursue "authentic existence, that is being open to the future and its possibilities. Inauthentic existence is being tied to the present, with all its vicissitudes, as if there is no better future."[6] Hell, then, is not a geographical place where individuals exist in anguish after death but is the experience of an inauthentic existence that includes living a broken and conflicted life.

One of Bultmann's interpreters expands on the implications of the theologian's view of hell: "In [Bultmann's] view, the 'final judgment' is not an event in history, but an event that takes place within the heart of each person as he or she responds to the call of God in each existential moment. Humans experience either heaven or hell in each moment."[7] We choose to live in heaven or hell depending on whether we choose to answer yes or no to God's call.

Paul Tillich and Correlation

Paul Tillich's theological method is known as correlation, which shares some common concerns with Rudolf Bultmann's approach to demythologizing. Both theologians seek to resolve their concerns about the distance between the biblical and modern worldviews, but in slightly different ways. These Christian thinkers share three related concerns. First, the language and concepts of the Christian tradition are often hard for modern people to understand. Second, although this tradition may be hard for people today to understand, it contains insights that can offer people life-giving interpretations of themselves and their situation in the world. Third, the Christian community needs to find ways of translating the language and concepts of the past into expressions and ideas that speak to people today. Bultmann zeroed in on demythologizing ancient myths. Although Tillich was sympathetic to this concern, he focused much less on the deficiencies of mythological worldviews and much more on broader differences in culture and language between the ancient world and today.

Tillich sought to help people today encounter the life-shaping power of Christian tradition through the method of correlation. In its fully developed form, this involves deep technical matters of philosophy and theology.[8] Although it is a complicated method, its essential components can be stated simply. He begins by acknowledging that individuals and communities struggle to understand the meaning of their present situation. Writing in 1951, Tillich almost seems prescient when he describes his time period in ways that could describe the world of the twenty-first century. He speaks of individuals and communities experiencing "the present situation in terms of disruption, conflict, self-destruction, meaninglessness, and despair in all realms of life." Tillich believed that people seek—and God intends—"a reality of reconciliation and reunion, of creativity, meaning, and hope."[9] Tillich calls this new mode of life the "New Being."

The current situation of tension and uncertainty raises profound questions for people who are battered by such a chaotic environment. Individuals and communities need the resources of tradition to make theological sense of their present experience and to live with hope toward the future, what he calls the New Being. Tillich calls particular attention to the Bible, voices from church history, and voices from the larger world as containing the perspectives that can open the way toward the New Being.[10] He seeks to correlate the resources of the tradition with the questions of the congregation and culture. That is, Tillich aims to identify specific elements in the tradition that speak to the questions and issues of the contemporary world.

The complicating factor, as we have indicated, is that the resources of the tradition are often cast in language and worldview that do not resonate fully with people today. Some of the meaning, perhaps even most, is lost on today's community because of changes in language and culture. Therefore, the interpreter needs to find contemporary modes of thought and expression that will be of use. First, the newer expression must interpret today's community in a manner similar to the way the earlier expression interprets people in antiquity. Second, communication needs to affect today's listening body in similar ways as the original expression affected people in an earlier and different world.

Tillich often made such correlations with language from psychology or philosophy, though a correlation could come from many other modes of understanding and communication. We see this phenomenon at work in one of Tillich's most famous sermons, "You Are Accepted." After describing the effects of sin as set out in the tradition, Tillich interprets the experience of sin for present-day people in terms of estrangement or separation. To be in sin is to be estranged.[11] God shows grace to the estranged and separated in the form of acceptance. Tillich rises to a mountaintop of language in describing this situation:

> Sometimes at that moment a wave of light breaks into our darkness, and it is as though a voice were saying: "You are accepted. You are accepted, accepted by that which is greater than you, and the name of which you do not know. Do not ask for the name now; perhaps you will find it later. Do not try to

do anything now; perhaps later you will do much. Do not seek for anything; do not perform anything; do not intend anything. Simply accept the fact that you are accepted!" If that happens to us, we experience grace.[12]

The experience of being accepted is the experience of grace.

A similar example of correlation is at work when Tillich speaks of hell. For much of the past, salvation was "salvation from hell in a future life."[13] Tillich, however, does not see hell as a geographical location beneath the earth where fire and sulfur belch for eternity:

> First of all, ["heaven" and "hell"] are symbols and not descriptions of localities; second, they express states of blessedness and despair. Third, they point to the objective basis of blessedness and despair, that is, the amount of fulfillment or nonfulfillment which goes into the individual's essentialization.[14]

For Tillich, the experience of New Being (as described above) is the experience of blessedness, and the experience of the present fractious state of the world points to despair. For Tillich, heaven and hell are not everlasting states of being but are part of an experience in "the eternal now."

When Tillich comments on the language of the wrath of God, we can see more clearly how this theologian understands hell. The "wrath of God," for Tillich,

> is the emotional symbol for the work of love which rejects and leaves to self-destruction what resists it. The experience of the wrath of God is the awareness of the self-destructive nature of evil, namely, of those acts and attitudes in which the finite creature keeps itself separated from the ground of being and resists God's re-uniting love.[15]

God does not actively condemn people to hell. As with Bultmann, human beings create the experience of hell by choosing against the New Being and choosing in favor of what we might call the old being, that is, the recalcitrant way things are.

For Tillich, then, the contemporary picture of the tradition's notion of hell is the suffering that we bring upon ourselves, as individuals and communities. This happens when we reject the possibilities of the New Being and cling to the old, even as the old ways turn the world into a chaos.

Before turning to the next chapter, we call attention to a phenomenon that complicates our discussion of these modernizing intentions, especially in some local congregations. Bultmann, Tillich, and many other interpreters sometimes speak as if everyone who lives in the Enlightenment/modern period subscribes to the modern point of view. However, many people have some ongoing vestiges of premodern attitudes in their thinking. Many Christians take full advantage of medical science—one of the hallmark achievements of modernity—while also embracing the traditional picture of hell as eternal fire and view modernizing hell in the way we have done in this chapter as being unfaithful to Christian theology, perhaps even being heretical.

Chapter 8

Voices Reclaiming Revelation

Barth, Brunner, and the Postliberals

At the end of the nineteenth century and moving into the early twentieth century, awash in scientific and technological advancements, the world—including theology—was optimistic about the future. Many theologians moved away from traditional authorities, such as the Bible and Christian doctrine, and began to pay more attention to other sources, especially human experience, including feelings. World War I destroyed many of these hopes, even as the science that seemed so promising at the beginning of the twentieth century contributed to the war's unparalleled death and destruction. Many of the leading theologians in Germany who had embraced the emergent liberal theology of the nineteenth century supported the German war effort. That expression of German nationalism led some younger theologians, including Karl Barth, to rethink their earlier embrace of this form of theological liberalism and seek an alternative view of God and the world. When Barth published his commentary on Paul's Letter to the Romans, arguing for a return to biblical foundations, it "fell like a bomb on the playground of the theologians."[1]

Theologians such as Karl Barth and Emil Brunner, who were Swiss citizens, along with others of similar mind began to question the legacy of the liberal theology of Friedrich Schleiermacher (see chap. 5), which emphasized religious experience. Instead, they turned to the Bible for guidance. While this movement has been called neo-orthodoxy, that name doesn't exactly fit. Its adherents weren't necessarily theological conservatives, but when it came to having something to preach, they found the theology of their teachers wanting.

In this chapter, we lay out a view of hell that emerged with Barth and Brunner and their theological heirs, who are often called postliberals. We start with the perspectives of Barth and Brunner before turning to their heirs (for our purposes we have chosen Daniel Migliore, Kathryn Tanner, and Joe Jones, all of whom address the question of salvation and divine judgment).

Barth's Hope of Salvation

The question of one's destiny fits into the theological category of eschatology (the doctrine of last things). While Barth (1886–1968) did not explore eschatology in detail, he left clues as to his views on this subject. Although he has often been placed in the universalist camp, he always denied this identifier. When he spoke of divine judgment and the question of hell, he tended to leave things open. He could envision the existence of hell but also imagine it being empty.

Barth's theological roots were in the Reformed tradition, a tradition that can be traced back to John Calvin and Ulrich Zwingli, and from there back to Paul through Augustine. With this background, he insisted that humanity would face the judgment seat of God because all are deemed transgressors. He could speak of God's wrath and even hell, which he defined in terms of self-chosen separation from God. While he moved close to universal restoration, he refused to embrace the concept.

Barth started with human transgression and divine wrath and resolved the question of divine judgment in Christ, in whom God meets humanity at the judgment seat. "He has borne our guilt, the suffering of the righteous wrath on our behalf." Therefore, "our sins are forgiven because He Himself has confessed and atoned for them in our place. This is the execution of the divine judgment."[2] However, he also insists:

> We can really comprehend that we are in the wrong before God only in the light of the fact that God will put us in the right in His judgment, that he is gracious to us in Jesus Christ, and not the reverse. As He actually addresses His love to us, He condemns us as transgressors and malefactors in the person of His

own Son. But we are acquitted and justified because, although this condemnation refers to us, it does so in the person of Jesus Christ, and therefore in such a way that what remains for us is forgiveness of sins.[3]

Whether Barth expected people to confess faith in Jesus to receive this blessing is not clear. In an interview at the Conference of the World Student Christian Federation in 1960, he says that when it comes to the destiny of those who are not Christians, he can't judge. He bears witness to Christ, and after that we will see what happens. As is often true with Barth, he doesn't give a conclusive answer.[4] When it comes to hell itself, in the same interview he says,

> Hell means to be in the place where you are once for all damned and lost without ceasing to exist, without losing the image of God, being what you are but being damned and lost, separated from God, whose creature you are, separated also from your neighbor, from the cohuman being, and separated in yourself— because there is such a thing as separation, a division, an opposition in our own existence. I think that what we are told about the fire of hell means this dissolution, this separation of man.[5]

Barth believed that since humanity has been created in the image of God, that image cannot be lost or destroyed. It does not appear that he would embrace annihilationism.[6] He assumes that humanity will stand before Christ, who serves as judge, but he also rejects the idea that hell should be part of the proclamation of the gospel. He tells his audience that "the proclamation of the gospel means the proclamation that Christ has overcome hell, that Christ has suffered hell in our place, and that we are allowed to live with him and so to have hell behind us."[7] Barth holds on to the idea of hell and doesn't believe that it should be part of the church's proclamation of the gospel, but isn't clear as to how one receives salvation.

The question then is whether Barth taught some form of universalism. He makes it clear that he does not embrace the concept of *apokatastasis,* the restoration of all things, although he acknowledges that it is a "very agreeable theory." Nevertheless, neither does he embrace the idea that a few will go to heaven while the majority go to hell. That is because Christ has overcome hell. Therefore, he states his belief that "we shouldn't try to solve this problem of the future automatically, but can only say: there is full salvation for all men in Christ; we are invited to believe in him, we want to do the best we can, and it shall be revealed to us before his judgment throne (cf. 2 Cor. 5:10) what we have done in our mortal life, good or bad."[8]

In an essay in *The Humanity of God,* Barth takes note of the message of Colossians 1:19, which speaks of God reconciling all things in Christ. In response to those who ask whether this means God is indifferent to human sin or moral lawlessness, he writes that "we have no theological right to set any sort of limits to the loving-kindness of God which has appeared in Jesus Christ."[9]

Barth affirms divine judgment, which is resolved in the death and resurrection of Christ. In an interview late in his life, when he was asked about the possibility of eternal life he intriguingly commented on both the reality of judgment and the possibility of salvation:

> Then we will see that he gave himself for the salvation of the entire world. For the sins of all humans, even Hitler's! I can't say that I understand it. And I understand even less that he died for my own sins—I'm better able to understand that he died for Hitler's. Anyone who knows even a little about sin cannot understand that my sins are forgiven me. In eternal life we appear as those who have been forgiven.[10]

Barth rejects universal salvation and the restoration of all things while holding on to the idea of hell, even if he believes it could be empty due to Christ's victory over hell. As to whether one must make a decision of faith, Barth told a group of Methodist preachers that "our temporal and eternal future does not depend on our decision but rather upon that which happened on Golgotha, and our decision of faith is our response to it." To say that one must respond as a condition for salvation would make the confession an achievement. But he's also not willing to say that everyone receives salvation. He can't even say that he is saved, for that is a matter of God's free grace.[11] Ultimately, then, for Barth the focus should not be on whether there is a hell, but on the promise that heaven is open. George Hunsinger summarizes Barth's position, which is similar to Karl Rahner's:

> Although Karl Barth is often labeled as a "universalist," he is best understood as standing in the tradition of holy silence. If a forced option is urged between the proposition "All are saved" and the counterproposition "Not all are saved," Barth's answer in effect is: "None of the above." Barth deliberately leaves the question open, though not in a neutral fashion, but with a strong tilt toward universal hope.[12]

Brunner's Call for Decision

Emil Brunner (1889–1966), like Barth, was a Swiss theologian who rejected the liberal theology of his teachers. Brunner took seriously the reality of sin and its consequences, and with that in mind, he sought to balance God's justice with God's love. In this regard, he warned against letting God's holiness get swallowed up by God's love.

Brunner speaks of the Last Judgment being the ultimate decision, which rests on a full disclosure of a person's being. He writes, "We shall stand naked and exposed, according to the truth of our being, with no concealing raiment." This act of judgment also serves as a point of separation or division, as seen in the parable of the Sheep and Goats (Matt 25:31–46). Thus, "it would contradict the whole Gospel tradition about Jesus to refer to the severity of the later church this conception—so odious to the modern man—of an ultimate discrimination and, by contrast, fearlessly to present the preaching of Jesus as being wholly concerned with the religion of love." In his view, there is no room for neutrality. One decides either for or against God.[13] He contrasts two solutions to the question of divine judgment, double predestination (Calvin) and *apokatastasis* or universalism (Barth), rejecting both. He is clear in his belief that the "Bible does not speak of universal salvation, but on the contrary of judgment and of a twofold destiny: salvation and doom."[14]

What he sought to do was hold God's love and holiness together, so that we might both fear and love God.[15] Brunner believed one must make a decision for God, which normally comes by way of the church's witness to Christ. To reject Christ leads to condemnation. He holds out hope that everyone might ultimately say yes. While he did not believe universal salvation was truly biblical, he could imagine everyone saying yes to God. That is the key for Brunner and the reason he rejected both double predestination and universalism. One must decide for or against God. The reason he holds out hope for the salvation of all people is that this is, according to the New Testament, the will of God, to reconcile all things in Christ (Col 1:20). Therefore, Brunner writes that "the question whether the possibility of the decision of faith is limited to this life, in view of 1 Pet 3:19, remains open."[16] It is not a definitive statement, but it holds out some hope.

Although he believes God desires the salvation of all humanity, he also believes that judgment is part of the biblical message, for judgment is "a necessary inference from the knowledge of the holiness of God."[17] When it comes to the punishment meted out by God, Brunner is a retributionist, holding that eternal punishment is not intended to reclaim the person. Most important is not the nature of the punishment but the reality of being eternally lost. Second, people are "disarmed from the outset . . . by the disclosure of a guilt for which no suffering would be too great a punishment, and by the revelation of love which takes from us the real punishment and pronounces us sinners free from guilt by grace."[18] While God's judgment has been passed on us, for humans are sinners, God's judgment is "transformed into His gracious promise, because the place of our missing righteousness is taken by the righteousness of Christ. In Him, the Crucified and Risen One, the Holy God acquits as 'righteous' by reckoning to us the righteousness of His Son; the God who does not let Himself be mocked, who unconditionally asserts His will, the God who, because He Himself is holy, wills that we also should be holy." Therefore, we are saved from God's wrath because Christ is our righteousness.[19] So, to the question of whether all might be saved, we have no answer. "The criterion of all true theology is this, that it should conclude with the words 'God be merciful to me a sinner' (Luke 18:13) and over and above that with this other word: 'But thanks be to God which giveth us the victory through our Lord Jesus Christ' (1 Cor. 15:57)."[20]

Postliberal Responses

When it comes to the legacies of Barth and Brunner, it is the former who has cast the largest shadow on the contemporary theological world. One expression of that legacy is known as postliberalism, a theological movement largely connected to Yale University, especially the work of George Lindbeck and Hans Frei. For our purposes, we are using this movement, which calls into question the theological tradition traced to Friedrich Schleiermacher, as a way of exploring ideas that descend from Barth and Brunner. Those connected with this movement seek to root their theologies in "the normative foundations of the tradition as these are articulated in the biblical narrative." Truth for them is measured by their faithfulness to the doctrinal core of the Christian tradition and, pointedly, not just by fit with a modern worldview.[21] We are using this movement (loosely) to draw together several figures: Daniel Migliore, Joe Jones, and Kathryn Tanner. We will give brief reviews of their views of the question of divine judgment and hell as a possible outcome.

Daniel Migliore (b. 1935), professor of theology emeritus at Princeton Theological Seminary, is a contemporary Reformed theologian with an interest in the work of Karl Barth. In his systematic theology, he frames the concept of hell not in terms of divine punishment but as a self-chosen resistance to or rejection of God's love, leading to isolation from God and others:

> Hell is best understood as wanting to be oneself apart from God's grace and in isolation from others. Hell is that self-chosen condition in which, in opposition to God's self-expending love and the call to a life of mutual friendship and service, individuals barricade themselves from God and others. It is the hellish weariness and boredom of a life focused entirely on itself. Hell is not the vengeful divine punishment at the end of history depicted by religious imagination. It is not the final retaliation of a vindictive deity. Hell is self-destructive resistance to the eternal love of God.[22]

Whether salvation is universal in nature or hell is empty cannot be answered with any definitiveness. Thus, he suggests we follow the lead of Karl Barth and Hans Urs von Balthasar and recognize that "it is best not to try to resolve this tension theoretically, but to hope and pray, on the basis of the super-abounding love of God in Jesus Christ, for a redemption of the world far greater than we are prone to desire or even able to imagine."[23]

Kathryn Tanner (b. 1957), professor of systematic theology at Yale Divinity School, insists that our salvation is assured if we are in Christ, who in the cross has done what is necessary to overcome sin and death, which is an act of grace.[24] When it comes to eternal life, she starts with the assumption that the eternal "is not the endless extension of present existence into an endless future, but a matter of a new quality of life in God, at the ready, even now infiltrating, seeping into the whole. Eternal life is less a matter of duration than a matter of the mode of one's existence in return to God, as that caliber of relationship itself in a new pattern for the whole of life."[25] Thus for her, eternal life is about more than what happens after death. Eternal life is a state of being that exists in the present, in that we live in God. She connects this reality called eternal life to our oneness with Christ "in a close relationship with him that allows us to draw upon what is proper to Christ as the divine Word incarnate."[26] In her view, we cannot operate independently of God if we are to experience this form of eternal life only because God holds up all that is. Tanner doesn't focus on what happens after death but on what happens in our current state of existence, which leads her to focus on the relationship between Christianity and economics. Thus, "the whole Christian story, from top to bottom, can be viewed as an account of the production of value and the distribution of goods, following this peculiar noncompetitive shape."[27] There is, in her view of things, a sense of universal relationship with creation that rests in the work of God in Christ, such that "the unconditionality of God's giving implies the absolute inclusiveness of God's giving: God gives without restrictions to everyone and everything, for the benefit of all."[28] As for whether hell exists or if it is populated, Tanner does not say. She offers her take on the various atonement theories in her book *Christ the Key,* but the focus is not on one's eternal destination but on one's relationship with God in Christ.

Joe Jones (1936–2022) was a minister in the Christian Church (Disciples of Christ) and a professor of theology and ethics at Christian Theological Seminary. Like others in this grouping, he studied at Yale Divinity School and was influenced by Barth and the linguist Ludwig Wittgenstein. He speaks of the idea of "dual destiny," in which some are destined for salvation and others are destined for damnation. While he affirms the Christian proclamation that people are called to respond to God's salvific work and leave their old lives behind and become a new creation, that does not resolve the question of the church's dual destinations.[29]

Having set up the question of humanity's ultimate destiny, Jones rejects the idea of dual destinies and opts for a single destiny, which is universal salvation. For Jones, salvation is a gift of God's grace. As for the Christian life, the concept of universal salvation need not undermine the call to love God and neighbor, for answering God's call does make a difference in the life of the Christian. Jones rejects the idea that God's judgment involves retribution. He writes that "God's *true and final judgment* has been expressed and revealed in the cross and resurrection of Jesus Christ and that it is the judgment of reconciling grace." Thus, in his death on the cross, "God takes the judged consequences of sin upon God's own triune Life. The righteousness and justice of God is that of redemption and renewal."[30]

Jones does speak of hell, but he envisions it being empty. He speaks of hell in terms of alienation from self, neighbor, and God, being the consequence of sin. However, hell as the ultimate destiny of some is a problematic idea. He asks whether this involves annihilation or eternal punishment. Since for God to consign someone to hell requires raising them from the dead, why not leave them dead (annihilation) and simply raise the righteous from the dead? As for eternal punishment, how does that square with Jesus' teaching on loving one's enemies? He writes that the "dominating theme of the NT—as I have continually argued—is the wonderfully saving grace of God in Jesus Christ, not the fear of hell and its ultimate occupation by real persons." Following up on that word, he points to the Apostles' Creed's statements about Christ's descent into hell, which he interprets to mean that Jesus emptied hell/Hades of its occupants. Thus, it was and remains empty. Jones draws on a Barthian phrase suggesting that "hell as absolute loss or everlasting punishment is an *impossible possibility*."[31]

If we think of Christian liberal theology as descending from Friedrich Schleiermacher, Barth, Brunner, and their heirs, three of whom we have discussed, seek to bring the question of divine judgment back into the equation. Barth leans toward universal salvation and the restoration of all things but doesn't fully embrace it, leaving it open even if ultimately hell is empty. Brunner makes it clear that the reality of sin demands a clear decision for or against God's offer of salvation in Christ, though whether there is room for a postmortem decision is left open. The more contemporary three theologians discussed here follow Barth in affirming the reality of divine judgment but keeping open the possibility that if hell exists it is empty. Thus, they hold out hope for a full restoration in Christ, but not without facing divine judgment.

Chapter 9

Voices of Eschatological Theologians

Käsemann, Moltmann, and Pannenberg

In the post–World War II era, a new generation of theologians emerged, who sought to move beyond the leading theologians of the previous era. We've looked at Protestant theologians such as Rudolf Bultmann, Paul Tillich, Karl Barth, and Emil Brunner. All four were in some ways connected, though they took different directions, as we've demonstrated. In this chapter, we look at three German theologians whose theologies all have an eschatological, even apocalyptic, dimension:[1] Ernst Käsemann (1906–98), Jürgen Moltmann (1926–2024), and Wolfhart Pannenberg (1928–2014). Käsemann (Lutheran) was the oldest of the three, a biblical scholar and Bultmann's student, while Moltmann (Reformed) and Pannenberg (Lutheran), both of whom have been connected to a theology of hope, were primarily theologians. All were Germans; Käsemann and Moltmann both served in the German army and spent time in Allied prisoner-of-war camps during World War II. It was in such a camp in Britain that Moltmann came to faith.

Ernst Käsemann

Käsemann is known for breaking with his teacher Rudolf Bultmann's emphasis on demythologizing the Bible and seeking to reclaim apocalyptic theology. His efforts would influence Moltmann and Pannenberg. His perspective on theology was deeply influenced by his experiences during World War II and even more importantly the death of his daughter Elisabeth at the hands of the

Argentinian junta in 1977. He defines the apocalyptic as "an event that begins with the Nazarene and finds its midpoint with the reigning Christ. Whoever reduces it to world-anxiety does so as if the rule and glory of Jesus Christ no longer existed in our time." The resurrection of the dead not only applies to "pious souls" but "is a revolutionary event alongside which all other revolutions appear harmless." When it comes to hell, he writes that it "simply lies distant from those who no longer allow themselves to be reminded, who in any case will not open their eyes and ears to the misery of Lazarus before their own door, or of those dying in distant lands."[2]

Käsemann's apocalyptic view of reality was rooted in the realities faced by a majority of humans in this world. His view was deeply influenced by his engagement with justice movements, especially in the developing nations. His understanding of hell was very much this-world oriented. In a 1980 essay, "The Eschatological Royal Rule of God," he reflects on the message of 1 John 5:19, which speaks of the world being "under the power of the evil one." While many in the developed world don't believe things are that bad, he writes that "we daily suppress the fact that, for the majority of its inhabitants, our earth is a hell; and we allow the truths that 'the light shines in the darkness' [John 1:5] and that Jesus died in no-man's-land to be mere pious phrases."[3] In an essay from 1981 titled "Where Eternal Life Begins on Earth," he writes, "The kingdom of God is not built on alms, however ready we are to give them. Hell cannot be exorcised with developmental aid, the capital of which flows back to us in interest. The White Man, even in religion and theology, is everywhere detested and hated by people of color because he wants eternal life already on earth at the cost of other creatures."[4] Käsemann not only speaks of hell as an earthly reality, but he also speaks of God's descent into this hell in Christ. He writes of Jesus that he not only became human but he "descended into the hell that earth is not yet for us today but certainly is for most of its inhabitants, and in which we are complicit, since we live at the cost of others. To believe means to hear that our God comes to us even in hell and thus will be called our Redeemer and Liberator."[5]

When Käsemann speaks of hell, he tends to speak in terms of what people, especially people in the developing world, who have been exploited by European and North American powers, experience in the present. The focus is not on something lying on the other side of the grave. As for salvation, he affirms the message of 1 Timothy 2:4, that God desires the salvation of all. But again, the focus is on the inbreaking of God's realm in this world, not the next. Thus, Käsemann writes: "This world rests on God's mercy. When powers and forces sever it from that mercy and subdue it under their yoke, the world becomes a hell, as more than half of all humans experience it today in body and soul." He writes further that "if divine mercy is despised as a basis for life, the demons gain power to ruin humanity worldwide, to make the cosmos the theater of war of all against all, and finally of universal suicide. We have been dragged far enough into this inferno. It is high time to be opened to the gospel."[6] The response desired by the God who enters the hell that exists on earth is for us to allow God to form us rather than trying to form God in our own image. That requires viewing the world through the cross.

Jürgen Moltmann

Jürgen Moltmann was a professor emeritus of theology at Tübingen University and one of the most important and influential contemporary theologians. Like Käsemann, who would later be one of his teachers and then a colleague, he experienced World War II as a soldier in the German army. While Käsemann was a member of the Confessing Church and had begun his academic career before being drafted into the army, the much younger Moltmann served at the end of the war and was captured and placed in a prisoner-of-war camp in Scotland, which is where he came to faith.

He is especially linked to what is known as the "theology of hope," a concept laid out in his first book, which carries that title. His theology is influenced by Ernst Bloch's *Principle of Hope* and is eschatological in nature in that it envisions an open future, wherein we live in anticipation of the coming of God's realm. For him, this future realm is not caught up in optimism but is rooted in God's promises that enable God's people, like Abraham and

Sarah and Israel in Egypt, "to risk the exodus into the unknown and to trust solely the star of promise."[7]

Moltmann writes that "the picture of the God who judges human beings in wrath has been the cause of much spiritual and psychological damage." It has led to people fearing death out of fear of hell. Some have responded to this by removing God from the equation, such that humans are responsible for being condemned to hell. If this is true, he writes, humans "are the masters of their own destiny, and God is only the executor or accomplice of the person's own decision. If he believes, God will take him to heaven; if he does not believe, God will send him to hell." In this concept, God becomes superfluous, and human freedom replaces "belief in God."[8]

Moltmann is rooted in the Reformed tradition; thus, he seeks to give God the lead role in the question of salvation. He finds both the idea that people damn themselves to hell and conditional immortality (annihilationism) unsatisfactory. Annihilationism is unsatisfactory because it removes those who do not believe from the experience of God's judgment. For Moltmann, judgment is related to justice, and the victims of injustice do not remain silent. Thus, "the expectation of the divine judgment which will bring about justice was originally the hope of victims of injustice and violence. The divine judgment was the counter-narrative and the counter-picture of the oppressed which was set over against the world of the triumphant perpetrators of violence."[9] Thus, there is a need for all humanity to face God's judgment.

According to Moltmann, Christ is the one who will serve as judge, and that judgment will rectify the realities of injustice. This will not involve retributive justice, such that the good are rewarded and the wicked are punished. Rather victims will receive justice, and perpetrators will be put right. Therefore, "victims do not remain victims forever and perpetrators do not have to remain perpetrators forever." Instead, perpetrators will be redeemed and transformed as through refiner's fire. He writes of this fire that "it is an image for God's love, which burns away everything which is contrary to God so that the person whom God has created will be saved."[10] For Moltmann, in the death and resurrection of Christ, our ultimate judge, hell is destroyed.

The goal is that "all disrupted conditions in creation must be put right so that the new creation can stand on the firm ground of righteousness and justice and can endure to eternity." This is a vision of a cosmic transformation of all things.[11] The question of whether all will be redeemed is resolved in "the Christian idea of universal salvation [that] is based on cosmic Christology, according to which 'death will be destroyed' (1 Cor 15:26) and hell annihilated."[12]

Ultimately the question of heaven and hell is rooted in one's view of God and God's purposes. He asks: "How can the God who loves what he has created condemn not just what is evil, destructive and godless in created beings but these beings themselves?"[13] When it comes to the Last Judgment, which Moltmann views positively, as a sign of hope rooted in the death and resurrection of Jesus, "the eschatological doctrine about the restoration of all things has these two sides: God's judgment, which puts things to rights, and God's kingdom, which awakens to new life."[14]

Wolfhart Pannenberg

Wolfhart Pannenberg was born two years after Moltmann, and he was not directly involved in World War II, unlike Moltmann and Käsemann. His theology, like theirs, has strong eschatological elements, but his perspective has few political elements. Not only is he less political, but he is also more conservative than the other two. What marks Pannenberg's theology is his attempt to ground his theological work in history, including the historicity of the bodily resurrection of Jesus. In his effort to ground revelation in history, he broke with Karl Barth, with whom he studied.

He grounded his view of eschatology (last things) in his belief in the coming of God to rule over creation. Regarding the Last Judgment, as Christoph Schwöbel notes, "Pannenberg's interpretation expresses that the participation of created beings in God's eternity requires their radical transformation. The point of divine judgment is not the annihilation of the world but its purification by the light of God's glory to enable its participation in God's eternal life."[15]

In his *Systematic Theology,* Pannenberg envisions God's judgment involving a refining fire, purging believers of everything that is "incompatible with the eternal God and with participation in his life."[16] As for the unbeliever, the one who chooses to stand aloof from Christ, he insists that God does not assign anyone to condemnation. "The word of Christ as the offer of salvation will then make clear that the lost drew the line themselves and separated themselves from salvation."[17] Because the majority of humanity have not been given the opportunity to receive the Christian message, "the event of a personal encounter with Jesus through the Christian message and a response of faith to it cannot be the universal criterion for participation in salvation or exclusion from it if we take seriously what the NT says about the love of God for the world that embraces all people."[18]

Humanity's exclusion from participation in the life of God is due to the hardness of the human heart. It is this exclusion from God's presence that "the ancient dogmas saw as the tortures of hell." As for the "individual features" ascribed to the idea of hell, he suggests that "as these have been delineated in so many pictures of the Judgment, [the idea] is certainly fantastic." He suggests that what these pictures say about the tortures of hell are inadequate descriptions of "the exclusion from communion with the living God." Shorn of these "horrific fantasies of an imagination running riot," theology must hold the "fundamental feature of the idea of hell": exclusion from being near to God "would be real hell." Thus, it is inappropriate to speak of hell as a place in time and space where the condemned suffer eternal torment.[19]

As to the advantage given to Christians, when it comes to the future judgment, they already know the standard for participating in eternal salvation. So, "believers move on to judgment with confidence because Jesus Christ, who became human and died on the cross for our deliverance and for our reconciliation with God, will be the standard of judgment."[20] Pannenberg, assuming God's love for all creation, offers a tantalizing vision of what appears to be a form of postmortem salvation. He does this by using the imagery of Christ's descent into hell as described in the Apostles' Creed. Pannenberg speaks less in terms of Jesus' sufferings and more of his triumph over death and hell. He points to 1 Peter 4:6, which speaks of Christ preaching to those in prison. This passage has long been interpreted as a reference to Christ preaching to persons residing in Hades. Pannenberg suggests that this passage might envision the possibility that Christ engaged in a form of missionary proclamation, such that those who had not heard or embraced Christ in life might have a chance to hear his message of repentance. He doesn't offer a guarantee of universal salvation, but he holds out the possibility that "all other men, too, even those who have died before Jesus' ministry, can achieve the salvation which appeared in him—even if in ways which are beyond our comprehension. The meaning of the Christian acknowledgment of the conquest of the kingdom of death and Jesus Christ's descent into hell lies in the universal scope of salvation."[21]

The three theologians discussed here start with an eschatological perspective that speaks in terms of the coming of God's realm or kingdom. Käsemann and Moltmann have more political elements in their view of last things, with a focus on God bringing about justice for the oppressed. This is especially true of Käsemann, who speaks of hell on earth. Moltmann envisions a final day of judgment where Christ reconciles all things, transforming both victim and perpetrator. While Käsemann is less interested in life beyond death, Moltmann holds on to that hope. Pannenberg also embraces a vision of the coming of God's realm that includes Christ's conquest of death and hell. Pannenberg's vision is more conservative, in part due to his desire to root the resurrection of Jesus in history. While Moltmann embraces a form of universal salvation, Pannenberg doesn't guarantee it. However, like the other two, he rejects the traditional picture of hell as a place in time and space.

Chapter 10

Voices from Liberation Theology

*T*he various forms of liberation theology start with praxis. That is, they start with human experience, especially the experience of oppression. We tend to identify liberation theology with movements of liberation in Latin America, which are focused on the liberation of the poor from oppression. However, there are various theologies of liberation that focus on experiences of oppression, such as Black, womanist, minjung, Palestinian, feminist, and queer theologies. While they may differ in many ways, largely due to differing experiences of oppression, they all focus their attention on life in the present. That is, liberation theologians may or may not envision otherworldly realities such as heaven or hell, but they will not be distracted by those possibilities when the needs of the present require attention. The concepts of heaven and hell, even in their otherworldly dimensions, are understood not as an escape from this life but as the foundation of hope for changing realities in the present world.

Most of the theological efforts on the part of liberationist theologians include the use of social analysis, whether Marxist or not. The reason for this type of analysis by theologians is to determine the nature of oppression and the means of overcoming it. The form of liberation desired depends on the situation at hand. Palestinian theologians discern a different form of oppression than do Latin American theologians, as they seek to navigate the realities of living under Israeli occupation. The concerns might be socioeconomic or racial-ethnic, but whatever the nature of oppression, the desire is to achieve justice for the oppressed. While Latin

American theology emphasizes the socioeconomic dimension of "God's preferential option for the poor," Brazilian theologian Clodovis Boff has called for a broadening of the concept of the "poor," since liberation theology is "the theology of the liberation of the oppressed—the liberation of their whole person, body and soul—and all of the oppressed—the poor, the subjugated, those who suffer discrimination and so on."[1]

These theologies do have an eschatological dimension—most speak of the coming reign of God—but because the focus is on liberating efforts in this life, less emphasis is placed on the afterlife and one's eternal destiny. Therefore, discussions of the concept of hell are largely absent. When spoken of, hell is not understood to be a place but rather a "state of experience." James Evans writes, "Heaven, in African American religious thought, usually refers to being in community with others, while hell is often described as a state of alienation, not only from God, but from others."[2] That is a state of being that exists in this life, which is the focus of God's liberating efforts, again in the present world. Liberationist theologies, whatever their context, tend to embrace a realized eschatology, such that the revealing of God's realm takes place in this life through movements of justice, especially on behalf of the poor and oppressed. Therefore, the *eschaton* (the day of judgment) has to do with the concrete historical liberation of the poor.

The Centrality of the Reign of God

Liberation theologies are eschatological because they emphasize the coming reign of God. However, they tend to define the reign of God in historical terms. J. Deotis Roberts, a Black theologian, writes, "The kingdom is present wherever the will of God is being done, individually and socially in *ethics* and *faith*."[3] Jon Sobrino, SJ, writes from a Latin American context: "An ultimate hope in a universal resurrection can be maintained, but the more urgent cry is for the coming of the Reign of God as such. . . . The Third World continues to stand in urgent need of liberation, and the best theological way to deal with liberation continues to be to do so in terms of the Reign of God."[4] Gustavo Gutiérrez speaks of the ethical dimension of God's realm. He writes that "the kingdom is a gift but also a demand. It is a freely given gift of God and it calls for conformity to God's will to life." He points to the Beatitudes serving as the church's Magna Carta, such that "our following in [Jesus'] footsteps finds expression in actions toward our neighbor, especially the poor, in life-giving works; in these, love of God and love of neighbor are intertwined and call for the other."[5] Leonardo Boff, a Brazilian Roman Catholic theologian, notes that when Jesus told Pilate that his reign is not *of* this world, he did not mean that his reign is not *in* this world:

> This radical dream, which demanded deep transformations, ran into harsh resistance from those upholding the established order of the time and brought down on Jesus curses, persecutions, and eventually a political and religious condemnation. That was indeed what happened with Jesus. But he took his dream to the end, to the point of undergoing the hell of the absence of God on the cross (Mk 15:34) and a sense of utter failure. However, the dream never dies.[6]

Note that Boff does speak of hell, but in terms of the abandonment of Jesus by God.

While Sobrino, Gutiérrez, and Boff speak out of a Latin American context, envisioning God's realm as having this-world relevance, James Cone speaks similarly out of the context of an African American experience. He writes that "the event of the kingdom today is the liberation struggle in the black community. It is where persons are suffering and dying for want of human dignity. It is thus incumbent upon all to see the event for what it is—God's kingdom."[7]

As Gutiérrez writes about God's realm, "the day of the Lord has arrived." By that he speaks not of *chronos* but *kairos,* such that God's realm has been revealed on earth, and not only as an interior reality. Therefore, "accepting the kingdom of God means refusing to accept a world that instigates or tolerates the premature and unjust deaths of the poor. It means rejecting the hypocrisy of a society that claims to be democratic but violates the most elementary rights of the poor. It means rejecting the cynicism of the powerful of this world."[8]

Defining Salvation

If liberationist understandings of God's realm have this-world implications, then the same will be true of liberationist understandings of salvation. Because salvation and God's realm are related, put simply, salvation begins with liberation from oppression in the present world. God is a God of hope, who, as James Cone notes, comes to "overthrow the powers of evil that hold people in captivity." He suggests that this is a prominent theme in the Black religious tradition, "with its claim that Jesus has not left black people alone in suffering."[9] When it comes to God's work of reconciliation, Cone writes, "If we take seriously the objective reality of divine liberation as a precondition for reconciliation, then it becomes clear that God's salvation is intended for the poor and the helpless, and it is identical with their liberation from oppression."[10] Therefore, when liberation theologians speak of salvation, it has political implications. To speak of Jesus as a savior is to envision him in his role as liberator, overcoming the powers and principalities—that is, the structures of society that oppress. Cone writes that "because God has liberated the oppressed from bondage, thereby making freedom possible, the oppressed must now accept their freedom by joining God in the fight against injustice and oppression."[11] Joining God in this fight for justice means working to change "the political, economic and social structures so that the distinctions between rich and poor, oppressed and oppressors, are no longer a reality among people."[12] For Cone, salvation is rooted in God's actions in Christ, but they are implemented through revolutionary actions, seeking freedom and justice, especially for those in the Black community.

Latin American theologians take a similar view of salvation. Gustavo Gutiérrez offers a definition of salvation that has similarities to Cone's, though the context is different. He speaks of salvation in terms of seeking liberation from oppression, including poverty, in this life. Writing in 1968, he comments, "If we understand salvation as something with merely 'religious' or 'spiritual' value for my soul, then it would not have much to contribute to concrete human life. But if salvation is understood as passing from less human conditions to more human conditions, it means that messianism brings about the freedom of captives and the oppressed, and liberates human beings from the slavery that Paul VI referred to."[13] In his seminal book, *A Theology of Liberation,* Gutiérrez writes that "salvation embraces all men and the whole man; the liberating action of Christ—made man in this history and not in a history marginal to the real life of man—is at the heart of the historical current of humanity; the struggle for a just society is in its own right very much a part of salvation history."[14] Sin is not individual or private, but a social and historical fact that is present in oppressive structures. This requires a radical form of liberation, which is understood in political terms. It is a salvific action, but not the entirety of salvation, which finds fullness in Christ. Gutiérrez envisions the church (he is Roman Catholic) being the sacrament of salvation and thus should reflect in its structures the salvation it proclaims: "As a sign of the liberation of man and history, the Church itself in its concrete existence ought to be a place of liberation."[15]

The Day of the Lord

The eschatological vision of liberation-oriented theologians is focused on the realities of this world and not the next. They may envision life after death, but that is not the focus. That being said, as James Cone writes: "Heaven cannot mean accepting injustice in the present because we know we have a home over yonder. Home is where we have been placed now, and to believe in heaven is to refuse to accept hell on earth. This is one dimension of the future that cannot be sacrificed." He insists that "Black theology cannot reject the future reality of life after death—grounded in Christ's resurrection—simply because whites have distorted it for their own selfish purposes."[16]

Salvation is an act of God in Christ, but it involves liberation from oppression, whatever form that oppression takes. Gutiérrez denies that salvation is otherworldly and that this life is essentially a test. Rather, "salvation—the communion of men with God and the communion of men among themselves—is something which embraces all human reality, transforms it, and leads it to its fullness in Christ."[17] José Comblin makes it clear, from a liberationist perspective, "the life of heaven is of interest as far as it offers a goal and a content for this life here on earth. Eternal life is of interest if it sets up a norm and a pointer to a better life here on earth."[18]

Therefore, even in the Last Judgment, as spoken of by Jesus in Matthew 25, the emphasis is on what happens now, with little said about hell. That does not mean liberationist voices do not speak of God's wrath. Turning again to James Cone, we read: "A God without wrath does not plan to do too much liberating, for the two concepts belong together. A God minus wrath seems to be a God who is basically not against anything. All we have to do is behave nicely, and everything will work out all right."[19] Again, while not speaking of hell, Cone makes it clear that wrath is an expression of God's love for the oppressed: "If God is a God of the oppressed of the land, as the revelation of Christ discloses, then wrath is an indispensable element for describing the scope and meaning of God's liberation of the oppressed. The wrath of God is the love of God in regard to the forces opposed to liberation of the oppressed." Thus, one need not speak of hell as a reality to affirm that wrath is part of God's identity.[20]

Liberation theologies in general do not reject the idea of the afterlife, but the focus is on liberation from oppression in the present. As James Evans writes from an African American perspective, the concept of universal salvation is alive within Black theology, and in liberation theology as a whole: "The cosmic dimension of hope points to the fact that God creates and redeems all that is. The multidimensionality of Christian hope in African American religious thought has its roots both in African traditional thought and in the Bible. Both suggest that hope is wholistic, intergenerational, and universal."[21]

Chapter 11

Voices from Open and Relational Theologies

We turn now to a rather broad movement known as open and relational theology. This title is now associated with a movement in which a prime mover is Thomas Jay Oord, whose approach to the afterlife we discuss below.[1] In addition, this designation describes two theological families that share important core convictions and yet differ at one crucial point. The two theological households are open theism and process theology (sometimes called relational theology). As is the case with virtually all other theological families, there are diverse approaches within these two major groups. As we identify the main ideas that open theism and process thought have in common, we note the major difference separating the two, as well as call attention to some representative approaches to the notion of hell associated with these families and with the broader open and relational theology stream.

Clark Pinnock, a noted open theist, succinctly summarizes similarities between open theism and process theology:

> We both reject the notion that God is an absolute being unaffected by the world. We both insist that God is love and therefore filled with compassion and sensitivity. We believe that the future is open and that some kinds of change even belong to the divine perfection and are not alien to it. We believe that God not only affects creatures but that creatures affect God. We both think that God suffers when things go badly for creatures. We both hold to the reality of libertarian freedom and consequently we both recognize that genuine evils exist. Both models are impressive ways to get at important things we both care a lot about.[2]

Key points of similarity for open theism and process theology are that God seeks the most loving possibilities for human life and for the world and that God does not immediately control what happens to individuals and the world. Oord refers to God's *uncontrolling* love.[3] The present and future are not predetermined. We determine the character of life in the present and future by the choices that we make in response to God's invitations. As Pinnock says, the future is open.

At another key point, however, open theism and process theology disagree. Open theism is an expression of evangelical theology which holds that God has absolute power and authority. Yet, for open theists, God voluntarily gives free will to human beings and other creatures. God has the power to intervene in this world and its affairs, and God controls what happens in the afterlife, but between now and whatever comes next, human life is a season of decision making.

By contrast, Oord, an open and relational theologian, believes that God does not have absolute power. To be sure, God does have more power than any other entity, but it is limited and operates by persuasion. God does not voluntarily choose to detach from life: God's power, by nature, is limited. Oord puts this dimension of God vividly in the title of his book *God Can't*.[4] God cannot simply step into history or the world beyond present history and reshape individuals and circumstances by singular acts of the divine will. God operates within the structures and patterns of the world. While divine power is limited, it is nevertheless omnipresent. In every situation, God is present to offer the highest possibilities for love within the limitations of the circumstance.

Open Theism and Preferences for Annihilation and Purgatory

These understandings come into play in attitudes toward hell in open theism. Many open theists join other evangelicals in believing that the holy God must punish sin to act justly. Since

God has decided not to control human life and the choices people make, it follows that some people make choices that violate God's purposes (sin) and that eventuate in the need for God to punish them. Many evangelicals view the universe mainly in contemporary scientific terms but continue to speak of heaven and hell as if they are distinct places—even if some evangelicals do not think these realms are literally "above" and "below." When it comes to punishment in the afterlife, open theists tend to frame their considerations in the categories we have already identified: the fiery pit where people spend eternity, annihilationism (conditionalism), and purgatory. Of these options, open theists lean toward annihilationism and purgatory. Clark Pinnock summarizes the issues:

> The question before us is whether Christian theology should contend that the wicked who are finally impenitent suffer everlasting, conscious punishment in body and soul, or whether they are more likely to be destroyed in the destruction of a second death? Will the fire of hell torment condemned souls endlessly, or will it destroy and finally consume them? Does God intend to grant the wicked immortality in order to inflict endless pain upon them, or does [God] will that the wicked, following the last judgment, should finally perish and die?[5]

Pinnock answers these questions in the negative. For him, the best option is annihilationism (conditionalism) because it satisfies the need for justice while limiting the violence for which God is responsible. Annihilationism is consistent with the notion of God as loving, compassionate, and sensitive; such a God would seek as little suffering as possible. Something similar could be said for purgatory, especially since it has the potential to transfer those who pass through it into the community of the saved.

For most open theists, then, the future is open and significantly shaped by the choices we make, including the choice to be for or against God. But at death, the second coming and final judgment, or some other point, human choices run out, and God chooses the future of the human being in the afterlife, based on the choices they have made during this life.

Multiple Possibilities in Open and Relational Theologies

Process theologians typically believe that God is by nature love and that God always acts in love for all concerned in every situation. Another hallmark of process conceptuality is its intent to interpret the Christian faith (and all other things) in ways that are compatible with scientific ways of understanding the world. The process community places great stress on empirical evidence—on what we can perceive to really happen—as a basis for deciding what is more and less possible while respecting the limitations of human awareness and recognizing that more is often going on than we can take in through the senses. Process thinkers do not think of heaven and hell as domains of space but more as modes of experience.

Some process theologians do not believe that human beings have a conscious afterlife. Because the self is embodied, when the body dies, consciousness ceases to function. According to these writers, human beings live on through the effects they have had in the world, but the dead themselves no longer have consciousness.

Many others committed to process theology do think that an element of the self, while no longer embodied, continues to be conscious beyond the grave. Given the permeating emphasis on love in process, it is not surprising that all process theologians with whom we are familiar reject the idea of an everlasting hell in which God actively punishes people in a fiery afterlife. However, as we look briefly at the work of three process theologians, we see variety in the way interpreters who envision an afterlife imagine what happens beyond death.

Clark M. Williamson approaches the subject like many other process thinkers. Drawing from Julian of Norwich, Williamson foresees universal salvation: "All will be well." The reason for this confidence is vividly expressed: "Although an earthly mother may allow her child to perish, our heavenly Mother Jesus can never allow us who are his children to perish."[6] Williamson looks with favor upon Gregory of Nyssa and Origen. For Gregory, the day will come "when no single being created by God will fail to achieve the [realm] of God."[7] For Origen, God will be "all in all" and there will "no longer be any contrast of good and evil, since evil nowhere exists."[8] Williamson does not speculate on the details of the afterlife but posits that "God's loving grace will ultimately triumph" because that is the logical outcome of God's unconditional love for all (including the natural world) and God's will for justice for all (including the natural world). He concludes, "It is a radical confidence that all will be well because underneath are the everlasting arms."[9]

Thomas Oord, who is mentioned at the beginning of this chapter as a prime mover in open and relational theology, sees God having limited power and working through uncontrolling love. Human beings must choose how to respond to the possibilities posed by that love. God cannot go against God's own loving nature and condemn people to eternal suffering. Death does not end human awareness and the possibility of choice. When we die estranged from God and in violation of God's intentions for love, God does not assertively punish us but pursues us with relentless love.[10]

Oord sees three guarantees of relentless love.

1. "The God whose nature is uncontrolling love will never stop loving us. . . . Because love comes first in the divine nature, God *cannot* stop loving us." Consequently, "the God of relentless love works for our well-being in the afterlife."
2. "Those in the afterlife who say, 'Yes' to God's love experience heavenly bliss." Oord is undecided about the nature of this bliss. It may be "in either a different (spiritual) body or as a bodiless soul." The important thing is that "those who cooperate with God's relentless love enjoy eternal bliss."
3. "God *never* stops inviting, calling, and encouraging us to love in the afterlife." Never. To be sure, "there are negative consequences that come from refusing love. But these consequences are self-imposed, not divinely inflicted." Because God has limited power, "God cannot prevent the natural negative consequences that come from saying 'No' to God's love."[11]

Oord's point of view does not automatically result in universal salvation. But it offers an everlasting hope that everyone can eventually say yes to the One of Uncontrolling Love.

Marjorie Suchocki goes into more detail with respect to what might happen in the afterlife: "Would it be so strange to think that upon death when there is no newly created consciousness in the continuation of our histories, we might experience ourselves in God as participants in God's own life?"[12] Assuming that human beings are alive in God as a consciousness that is aware not only of itself but of God and of other consciousnesses that are alive in God, the "place" where this phenomenon takes place is the consciousness of God.

Given this version of the afterlife, Suchocki supposes the possibility of a three-phase process that functions as a kind of gentle version of purgatory that accounts for the violations of divine purpose committed by the self while opening the way for the consciousness of the self to experience fully and everlastingly the unmediated love and grace of God.[13] The self can pass through this proceeding because it takes place in the absolute love and security of God.

- In the first phase, people come to complete awareness of what they have been and done. They come face-to-face with the ways they have undercut God's larger purposes.
- In the second phase, people feel the effects of their attitudes and behaviors on others. They experience the experience of others: "Through the power of the divine sensitivity, each is mediated to the other, knowing oneself through the heart of the other. Joys that were given will be experienced; alternatively, the same dynamics mean that pains that were inflicted will also be experienced."[14] People in this phase realize the harm they have done. But one is not trapped forever in such a moment.
- The third phase is redemptive. Through love and grace, God brings all feelings, including the most painful recognitions of the harm one has done to oneself and others, into the fullness of God: "From the point of view of God, it is a movement into integration, whereby the many feelings . . . are brought into increasing modes of harmony."[15]

Suchocki asks directly, "How is there redress?" How does this process speak to the judge who condemned a woman to be burned at the stake and to the woman herself? Consider the woman and the judge. She is aware of him experiencing her pain within the divine nature. But her own movement is beyond that pain into transformation. The judge is not locked into her pain any more than she is; the judge too experiences her transformation in God and therefore participates in that transformation. She contributes to his redemption. The judge moves from alienation from others to integration in God and with others.[16] In this way, a violator does not, as one of our Bible students said, "get off scot-free." The penalty, so to speak, is to experience in oneself the violation of God's purposes that one has inflicted on others. But experiencing the penalty is not the end. God's omnipresent desire is to bring all entities into relationships of mutual support: "The edges of God are tragedy through the feelings of pain in the universe, but they are the edges only. The mighty center toward which we move in judgment is the overcoming of evil through its transformation by the power of God. In the center of God, the many are one everlastingly."[17]

Bob and Ron have been in study groups in which some of the participants express severe reservations about open and relational (including process) perspectives. To some students, open, relational, and process conceptualities do not maintain enough traditional perspectives on God—especially God's unlimited power. Thinkers in these schools of thought reply that they seek ways of understanding God that are consistent both with their deepest moral convictions about the nature and purposes of God (pure, unbounded love) and with their observations about what actually happens in the universe. Moreover, those who adhere to process, open and relational perspectives point out that their viewpoints do provide for accountability for individual and communal violation of God's purposes but in frameworks that can be ultimately redemptive. Those who partake of these worldviews recognize that our direct knowledge of the things of God is always incomplete, but they find their theology seriously believable amid the intellectual and social currents of the early twenty-first century.

Part 4

Voices Summarizing Three Main Views of Hell Today

We have journeyed from the worlds of the Bible across twenty centuries of voices from different times, different lands, different cultures, and different theological visions. In fact, we have reviewed so many perspectives on hell that the reader might feel overwhelmed. So, before turning to the study guide and to the task of sorting out how readers relate to the various voices as part of clarifying what makes sense to believe about hell, we offer a brief summary of four main voices in the churches on hell today. Participants in discussions about hell are likely to encounter these points of view, and it can be handy to have a basic map of their individual content and how they are related.

While aspects of these perspectives occur in the material already discussed in the book, we set them out here in sharp relief so that readers can see each perspective in its distinctiveness along with its strong points and the points about which some Christians have hesitations.

- Chapter 12 explores anticipations of eternal conscious punishment as either burning in flames or something worse.
- Chapter 13 explains an approach called annihilationism or conditionalism, which teaches that suffering punishment is cut short by the destruction or annihilation of a disobedient or unsaved person.
- Chapter 14 turns to universalism, the idea that everyone will be saved.

Interpreters who move in the first two streams (chaps. 12 and 13) focus on hell as a reality that takes place in an afterlife. While those who hold these positions manifest diversity in their understandings of hell, they believe in significant correspondence between statements about hell and what really happens to people. For example, human beings in the afterlife actually burn. Others believe that the self (including consciousness) is literally annihilated.

The notion of universal salvation discussed in chapter 14 typically presumes an afterlife in literal terms. Salvation means being saved from some form of afterlife punishment and saved into an afterlife of a new world. Notions of the afterlife world can vary widely, from conventional pictures of heaven where people reunite with loved ones, wear white robes, play harps, and pick fruit from trees, to a new realm of love, justice, peace, dignity, freedom, and abundance.

Although the majority of Christians, as well as religious Jews and Muslims, embrace one of these three primary approaches to hell—eternal torment, annihilationism (conditionalism), and universalism—there are many Christians, Jews, and Muslims who do not believe in an afterlife, whether heaven or hell. They may, however, use the term "hell" in a metaphorical or figurative way to speak of horrific experiences in this life. As a practical matter, any time readers encounter discussion of hell, we counsel asking the basic question, "What is the view of hell operating here?" Such a question can be focused on such things as reading material, voices in conversation, sermons, Bible study groups, doctrinal statements, and digital communications.

Chapter 12

Voices on a Literal Hell That Continues Forever

*W*hen the idea of a literal hell comes up in conversation today, our impression is that many people picture a place burning hot with flames, with the smell of sulfur fouling the air. Disobedient people who inhabit hell writhe in pain as they burn forever but are never consumed. While many people think of literal hell in this way, another large body of Christians conceive of hell as a literal reality that is made up of modes of punishment other than suffering in an eternal fire.

Hell as a Literal Place of Fire

John Walvoord, a widely respected interpreter, speaks for many who consider a fiery hell to be a literal reality. Walvoord asks: "Is the fire of eternal punishment to be understood literally?" He gets straight to the point in his answer: "In the attempt [by some people] to alleviate some of the suffering of eternal punishment, the question is naturally raised as to whether the fire of eternal punishment is literal. However, the frequent mention of fire in connection with eternal punishment [in the Bible] supports the conclusion that this is what the Scriptures mean. . . . There is sufficient evidence that the fire is literal."[1] While the fire itself is a central reality, the punishment is "partly mental, partly physical, and partly emotional." Indeed, hell is a domain of "mental anguish." And "there is no indication [in the Bible] of genuine repentance in hell."[2] The reason that God consigns some to hell is simple. "God is a God of infinite righteousness as well as infinite love."[3] God "demands absolute justice of the wicked."[4]

Walvoord acknowledges that human perception of the everlasting actuality of hell can never be complete. Yet, "eternal punishment is an unrelenting doctrine that faces every human being as the alternative to grace and salvation in Jesus Christ." Some people who hold this viewpoint do so arrogantly, condemning to eternal torment those who have not made a confession of faith in Christ or who otherwise fall into a category that they regard as disobedience. However, Walvoord makes it clear that such behavior is inappropriate. The potential that some people might be condemned should be a "spur to preaching the gospel, to witnessing for Christ, to praying for the unsaved, and to showing compassion on those who need to be snatched as brands from the burning [fire]."[5]

Hell as a Literal Experience of Suffering but Not through Fire

At the same time, many other believers who affirm the idea of a literal hell do not think that hell is a place of fire. A starting place for many who hold this viewpoint is articulated by another interpreter: "The writers of the New Testament were not concerned so much with the exact nature of hell as they were with the seriousness of the coming judgment. . . . The New Testament pictures of hell are metaphors and not literal descriptions."[6] The language of "fire" is symbolic; "the writers used the most powerful symbols available in the first century to communicate their meaning."[7] The suffering is everlasting, and if it takes place through means other than fire, that does not diminish its gruesomeness: "The images we find are shocking, and . . . the intent is clear. Hell is a place of profound misery where the wicked are banished from the presence of God."[8]

James I. Packer, an influential twentieth-century evangelical thinker, asserts that the reality of the literal hell is even worse than the metaphorical language of fire might suggest. Packer cautions: "Do not try to imagine what it is like to be in hell. . . . The mistake is to take such pictures as physical descriptions, when in fact they are imagery symbolizing realities . . . far worse than the symbols themselves."[9] Packer expands on the conditions in hell, saying that they include "loss of all good, all pleasure, all rest, and all hope; exclusion from God's [favor] and exposure to his anger; remorse, frustration, fury, despair; self-hate as a form of self-absorption; introversion to the point of idiocy."[10]

Packer reviews a series of images of hell in the New Testament that include incineration, fire and darkness, weeping and gnashing of teeth, destruction, and torment, and concludes that they depict "total distress and misery." He continues:

> If, as it seems, these terms are symbolic rather than literal (fire and darkness would be mutually exclusive in literal terms), we may be sure that the reality, which is beyond our imagining, exceeds the symbol in dreadfulness. New Testament teaching about hell is meant to appall us and strike us dumb with horror, assuring us that, as heaven will be better than we could dream, so hell will be worse than we can conceive. Such are the issues of eternity, which need now to be realistically faced.[11]

He concludes, "The reality . . . will be more terrible than the concept; no one can imagine how bad hell will be."[12]

We continue to hear some people disparage perspectives such as those represented by Walvoord and Packer as being insensitive and uncaring. However, both Packer and Walvoord understand the hard edge of their comments as pastoral expressions of care for those who have not come to evangelical faith. Packer says, "The purpose of Bible teaching about hell is to make us appreciate, thankfully embrace, and rationally prefer the grace of Christ that saves us from it (Matt 5:29–30; 13:48–50). It is really a mercy to mankind that God in Scripture is so explicit about hell. We cannot now say that we have not been warned."[13]

From the standpoint of those who hold literal views of hell, the preacher and teacher who call the attention of the congregation to the possibility of hell are like the parent who sees the small child in the kitchen mesmerized by the flashing blue, yellow, orange, and red colors in the flames coming from the gas burner under the Dutch oven on the stove. As the child reaches for the flames, the parent cries out, "Stop! Stop!" The cry, with its hard edge, is intended as an expression of love. To the degree that the cry frightens the child, it is intended to prevent harm. Many people who hold literal views of hell and communicate them to others are not hard-hearted or mean. They speak not only because God wants them to do so, but out of concern for others.

Chapter 13

Voices on Annihilationism

An Alternative to Continuous Punishment in Fire

A group of interpreters who reject eternal conscious torment, but do not embrace universal salvation, believe that the wicked and possibly nonbelievers will face divine judgment as annihilation, or terminal punishment. This concept, sometimes called conditionalism, may retain elements of a literal hell, including fire, but it assumes that whatever punishment God metes out will not be eternal. Some, following Edward Fudge, insist that those cast into the lake of fire by God will be consumed by the flames, experiencing permanent extinction.[1] This may include intense suffering, but it will be brief and will lead to their annihilation and loss of consciousness. Those holding this position seek to balance God's love and justice; in their minds, a loving God cannot consign human beings to eternal conscious torment. Clark Pinnock, one of the more prominent proponents of this point of view, points toward one of the starting points of the concept of annihilationism. Someone "asks, as I do, how anyone can preach a doctrine that says God condemns people to suffer forever in literal flames. As if God would make sinners like chestnuts roasting on an open fire!"[2]

Pinnock offers a poignant perspective:

> How can one reconcile this doctrine [that God inflicts eternal suffering on sinners] with the revelation of God in Jesus Christ? Is he not a God of boundless mercy? How then can we project a deity of such cruelty and vindictiveness? Torturing people without end is not the sort of thing the "Abba" Father of Jesus would do. Would God who tells us to love our enemies be intending to wreak vengeance on his enemies for all eternity?[3]

John R. W. Stott notes, similarly, "Emotionally, I find the concept [of eternal suffering] intolerable and do not understand how people can live with it without either cauterising their feelings or cracking under the strain."[4] However, Stott acknowledges, "Our emotions are a fluctuating, unreliable guide to truth." While Stott is aware of his emotional predisposition, his question is not "what does my heart tell me, but what does God's word say?" For Stott, a leading evangelical, the Bible is the key to "God's word."[5] Like others in this movement, he interprets the pertinent biblical passages to speak of annihilation rather than eternal conscious torment. Questions about punishment by a merciful God raise the possibility of reexamining the tradition, but annihilationists cannot recommend their viewpoint unless they believe it is warranted by Scripture.

In addition to considering the biblical witness—and concluding that it points to annihilation—Pinnock raises a moral argument:

> What does this tradition [of eternal suffering] do to the moral goodness of God? Torturing people forever is an action easier to associate with Satan than with God, measured by ordinary moral standards and/or by the gospel. And what human crimes could possibly deserve everlasting conscious torture?[6]

Pinnock puts it hauntingly: "Everlasting torture is intolerable from a moral point of view because it pictures God acting like a bloodthirsty monster who maintains an everlasting Auschwitz for his enemies whom he does not even allow to die. How can one love a God like that?"[7]

In the face of such profound objections to the notion of a literal hell of everlasting punishment, why do Pinnock and other annihilationists believe that some form of punishment—albeit more humane—is necessary? The answer is that people have the freedom to choose to live according to God's designs for faithfulness and blessing or to live in violation of God's aims because they are more attracted to the possibilities offered by the unfaithful, violating life. Some people choose the path that leads to destruction.

For many annihilationists, God would like to save all people, but God does not override human freedom. So, "God is morally justified in destroying the wicked because God respects their human choices. He will not save them if they do not want to be saved. . . . The God who seeks our well-being in fellowship with [Godself] will not force that friendship upon anyone. In the end [God] will allow us to become what we have chosen."[8]

Moreover, annihilation is more consistent with proportional justice. Indeed, John Stott says, "The belief that God will judge people 'according to what they [have] done' (e.g., Revelation 20:12) . . . implies that the penalty inflicted will be commensurate with the evil done."[9] Consigning people to suffer forever, whether in flames or in some other way, is a disproportionate punishment for most violations.

Although some people believe everyone has an afterlife—perhaps a soul that lives on after death either in heaven or in hell—annihilationists believe that the saved become immortal and continue to live with God forever while the unsaved perish altogether. Living beyond death is conditioned upon belief in Jesus Christ. Rather than being subjected to never-ending torment, those who do not receive immortality simply cease to exist, though not until facing God's judgment. Thus, as Terrance Tiessen writes, "Immortality is conditioned upon faith, hence unbelievers will experience not incorruption, immortality, and endless life, but death of body and soul. As a way of describing the end of the wicked, *annihilation* puts its emphasis on that end itself."[10]

To put it another way, immortality is conditional; it is not a constituent part of human life. Proponents of this view reject the concept of an immortal soul as an unbiblical import of Greek philosophy into Christian theology. Immortality is a gift of God to those who are saved by Christ. They alone will experience immortality and live forever in the presence of God. Those who choose not to avail themselves of God's grace in Christ will perish. As John Stackhouse writes:

> Unlike the case of words translated "eternal," when the Bible speaks of something being "destroyed" or something experiencing "death," it generally means termination. And, as Edward Fudge has assiduously demonstrated, the Bible is replete with passages—literally dozens and dozens—that speak of the destiny of the lost as termination, end, disappearance, eradication, annihilation, and vanishing.[11]

Thinkers in this stream do not pretend to have a full view of everything that happens on the route to final destruction. As to whether God metes out degrees of punishment on the way to final extinction, Clark Pinnock writes, "I am not exactly sure how to answer that because it requires more detailed knowledge of the precise act of damnation than we have been given. I am sure it is not beyond God's wisdom to figure out how degrees of punishment might enter into this event. Maybe there will be a period of punishment before oblivion."[12]

To conclude, proponents of conditionalism/annihilationism, while they may differ in degree, seek to hold in tension a belief in divine judgment, possibly including the existence of hell, with God's love and compassion, while at the same time not embracing universal salvation. Those who hold this view would also deny that God sends anyone to hell, even if temporarily, but rather that it is a chosen destiny. As Chris Loewen puts it, "Hell is not merely a place one goes to, but most importantly, it is the *telos,* the natural consequences of choosing a life apart from God. In the language of Conditional Immortality, Hell is when the offer of life is forever removed from their reach."[13] That is, they experience extinction.

Chapter 14

Voices on Universal Salvation

*I*n the introduction to part 4, we call attention to the importance of getting a clear picture of ideas operating in discussions about hell. When it comes to universal salvation, this is especially important. Some people use this phrase to indicate that God offers salvation to everyone; God does not withhold the possibility of salvation from anyone, but people must accept this offer. By contrast, in this chapter universal salvation refers to God actually saving every person. God does not just offer the possibility of salvation, but God actually saves everyone.

Universal salvation (sometimes called universalism) comes in many forms. Robin Parry articulates a widespread Christian understanding of universal salvation: "Christian universalism is the view that in the end God will reconcile all people to himself through Christ."[1] However, not all universalists believe that universal salvation comes about through Christ. Some believe that God saves in other ways. Moreover, proponents of universal salvation sometimes differ in the ways they understand salvation itself, but they agree that everyone will be included in God's realm in the end.

Proponents of universal salvation are averse to the concept of hell as the place of eternal conscious torment, as advocated by proponents of conditional immortality.[2] They are also averse to the idea of annihilationism.[3] Proponents of universal salvation go a step further than conditionalists and embrace some form of universal restoration of all persons and even all creation, though some allow for some form of punishment or purgation.

At the heart of the argument in favor of universal salvation or restoration of all things is the belief that God is, by nature, love. If God not only loves the world but is love itself, then it is inconceivable that God would either consign someone to eternal conscious torment or even extinguish their life. Robin Parry writes: "Now the Christian instincts here are simple and clear: if God is love then God loves all his creatures. And to love someone is to want the best for them. For a human creature, the best—from a Christian perspective—would be union with God through Christ. So it seems clear that if God is love then God will at least desire to bring all people into union with him (which in a sinful world will require salvation from sin)."[4] We see this perspective present in John Hick's argument for universalism: "We shall find incredible and even blasphemous the idea that God plans to inflict perpetual torture upon any of his children. . . . [Someone] could with a good conscience attribute to God an unappeasable vindictiveness and insatiable cruelty which would be regarded as demonic if applied analogously to a human being."[5] John A. T. Robinson adds, "Judgement can never be God's last word, because if it were, it would be the word that would speak his failure."[6] While universalists come to their rejection of both eternal suffering and annihilation from many different directions, they tend to share the belief that it is a contradiction to think a loving, compassionate, merciful, and gracious God would sentence people to eternal conscious torment. Some people in the universalist camp, such as Origen, do think a period of purification may take place between death and the final entry into salvation (on Origen, see chap. 4).

As we noted earlier, Christians are sometimes surprised to learn that universalism has been present in the church almost since the beginning. Chapters 4 and 5 call attention to the presence of impulses toward universalism as early as the second and third centuries, with Origen (185–254 CE), Gregory of Nyssa (335–395 CE), Maximus the Confessor (580–662 CE), and Isaac of Nineveh (613–700 CE) at least entertaining such an idea. Some mystics in the eighteenth century believed that all would be included in the universal restoration.

Beginning in the late seventeenth century, the Enlightenment created an environment in which individuals and communities could more easily embrace the possibility of universal salvation. These perspectives included respect for reason and science, as well as the decrease in the automatic submission to traditional interpretations of the Bible, Christian doctrine, and ecclesial leaders. They included the idea of human rights that gave the individual freedom to be self-determining. The Enlightenment posited tolerance for different religious viewpoints. Many of these qualities continue into the post-Enlightenment (or postmodern) world of today. Although many people embraced Enlightenment perspectives, many others continued traditional patterns of thinking—as do many people today.

Ideas resonant with universalism grew more numerous in the Enlightenment world and sometimes took communal expression, even eventuating in the formation of churches whose distinctive beliefs included universal salvation, often known as Christian universalism. The Universalist Church in the United States was founded in 1774, for example, in no small part to promote the notion of universal salvation.

A generation ago, Richard Bauckham observed that since the Enlightenment period, "No traditional Christian doctrine has been so widely abandoned as that of eternal punishment." The number of formally trained theologians who advocate the doctrine of eternal punishment appears to Bauckham to be diminishing: "The alternative interpretation of hell as annihilation seems to have prevailed even among many of the more conservative theologians." Bauckham believes that among less conservative thinkers, "universal salvation, either as hope or as dogma, is now so widely accepted that many theologians assume it virtually without argument."[7]

While Bauckham may be generally correct that the tides of scholarly interest have receded in matters related to hell and universal salvation, our experience—as indicated in the introduction to the book—is that these topics are still of interest for many Christians. Indeed, significant works continue to appear and be discussed in personal conversations, church groups, and social media.

One of the most visible demonstrations of continuing interest in the question of hell and whether everyone might eventually be restored to fellowship with God is the work of David Bentley Hart, whose book *That All Shall Be Saved* (2019) has struck a chord with many people.[8] Hart, writing from an Orthodox Christian perspective, objects to the idea of both eternal punishment and annihilation. After reviewing these and other attempts to take some of the onus off God as the owner and operator of hell, Hart concludes, "Not a single one of these attempted justifications for the idea of an eternal hell actually improves the picture of God with which the infernalist orthodoxy presents us, and it is this that should be the chief concern of any believer."[9]

Instead, Hart follows Gregory of Nyssa in conceiving the doctrine of creation from nothing as the ground for asserting that "all shall be saved" (on Gregory, see chap. 4), stating, "The end toward which he acts must be his own goodness; for God is in himself the beginning and end of all things." It would be a contradiction to say that God would sentence anyone to an eternity of suffering. For God is not only the beginning of all things but also the end of all things. God reveals God's "goodness in making the world."[10] Hart rises to poetry as he enlarges on this theme:

> In Christ, . . . this triumph will be fully realized only when God is "all in all"—in the sense both that God will be "over all things" and that God will be "within all things" (including every rational will)—and when creation, by this perfect union with God, is finally fully raised up out of the nothingness from which God liberates it in making it exist.[11]

Hart allows that there may be some form of punishment on the way to the life to come. However, such punishment would be "merely the final purgative purification of every soul—like the cautery or knife wielded by the surgeon, or like the implement for stripping clay from a rope."[12] At the same time, Hart does accept a form of hell: "As it happens, I do believe that the only hell that could possibly exist is the one of which those Christian contemplatives speak: the hatred within each one of us that turns the love of others—of God and of neighbor—into torment. It is entirely a state that we impose on ourselves."[13]

Many thinkers in the recent past and today embrace some form of universalism, even the view that God seeks the salvation of all humankind not only in the hereafter but more specifically in the present. This concern is important to many communities in our time in ways similar to the concern for salvation from hell in earlier times, as it emphasizes God's hope and blessing among all. This impulse reaches from concern for the well-being of individuals and communities through justice, respect, mutual support, peace, and material sustenance, as well as for the well-being of the creation itself. For those who continue to believe in universal salvation in the afterlife, the affirmation of universal salvation contributes to the well-being of the moment today because it frees people from being anxious about what lies beyond so that they can invest fully in efforts to respond to God's invitation toward inclusive well-being in the present.

We note one key challenge to the idea of universal salvation: the role of free will. If everyone and everything is restored, does this not overrule free will? While such a question might not worry a person coming from a tradition that affirms predestination—that is, God makes the final call—what about those who seek to preserve the right of a person to refuse God's offer of salvation? That is, God may desire to save everyone, but perhaps not everyone wishes to be saved. Robin Parry answers that concern by suggesting that God can and will reveal to a person the truth in such a compelling way that in the end, everyone will embrace God's offer of salvation:

> So, from this point of view, God simply needs to work in many and various ways (even in hell) to gradually increase awareness of the truth of the situation. The greater our Spirit-enabled appreciation of that truth, the greater will be our desire to choose God and the lesser will be our desire to reject God. Of course, short of an overwhelming revelation, we could still theoretically reject God. Only at the point at which we are fully informed could we no longer reject God, and I doubt that many people would need to get to that stage before choosing God. But even if we are fully informed, we are still free.[14]

How this might happen is answered in various ways, but the assumption is that in the end, God will reconcile all of creation.

Afterword

*W*hen we published *Second Thoughts about the Second Coming,* we did not include a statement of what we—Bob and Ron—believe about the second coming. Almost every time we have discussed that book, however, people have asked us, "What do *you* believe?" In this short afterword, we each respond to that question. There are both similarities and differences in our thought processes and conclusions, which we have discussed as we have worked on this project. While we may have differences at certain points, what we have written to this point is based on a consensus between the two of us. What we have written in this afterword reflects our personal perspectives and experiences.

What Does Ron Believe?

I (Ron) grew up in a county-seat congregation of the Christian Church (Disciples of Christ) on the edge of the Ozark Mountains in southern Missouri. The congregation was moderately conservative and did not emphasize the possibility of hell as an afterlife destination. The emphasis in our congregation was on God's love and on living in that love in our day-to-day interactions.

I was born in 1949 and was raised in the mind-set of modernity, that is, thinking that we establish truth through empirical verification. Science was not a god, but it was highly respected. Moreover, the Disciples tradition emphasizes a rational approach to faith. The teacher of our high school Bible school class said, "You want a faith that makes sense." Although he might not have put it this way, he meant a faith that is logically coherent and consistent with the modern worldview. The original *Interpreter's Bible* had been published only a few years earlier, and he regularly brought volumes to class so we could have access to what he considered the best of current scholarship. He encouraged questions and introduced us to the possibility of different interpretations of the Bible.

Not surprisingly, two of the big questions for me were (1) what to make of things happening in the biblical world that did not happen in my world (e.g., the ax head floating on the water in 2 Kgs 6:1–7), as well as (2) what to make of the claim that I heard at the Lord's Table every week that "God is love," in the face of the continued suffering in the world and descriptions in the Bible of God doing horrific things, punishing people for disobedience. Although our church did not talk about hell, I ran across it while reading the New Testament, and I wondered in a low-intensity way if it was possible to reconcile the God of whom we sang "pure, unbounded love, Thou art," and God consigning people to the place "where their worm never dies and the fire is never quenched" (Mark 9:48).[1]

These questions lingered even as I prepared for the ministry in college and seminary. In undergraduate school, I discovered demythologizing, as described in chapter 7. This approach often made it possible to honor what a text asked people to believe and do in antiquity and to find meaning for today by separating the husk and the core—that is, by peeling away the elements of the ancient worldview while identifying the core values that transcended that worldview. I might not believe that an ax head floated, but I could believe that the story teaches that God strengthens us so we can confront forces that oppose God's values and practices. Helpful as it was, this approach did not resolve all issues, especially the tension between thinking that God is love and living in a world of so much suffering. To be honest, I did not give a lot of thought to whether God might condemn people to weeping, wailing, and gnashing of teeth, but the issue did not go away.

In college and seminary, I was introduced to significant aspects of the modern worldview (see chap. 11). At the risk of oversimplification, I condense a network of complicated ideas into a few sentences that describe why I came to reject the idea that God sends people to hell, whether hell is conceived as a fiery pit or in some other way, and why I came to embrace the possibility of universalism.

- A good many Christians believe that God is simultaneously altogether loving, altogether powerful, and altogether just.
- However, to the mind of other Christians, God cannot be altogether loving *and* altogether just while consigning people to punishment in the afterlife. For God to send people to suffer in hell, whether for eternity or temporarily for some form of purgation, would indicate that God's love is limited and that God's desire for justice (in the sense of making people pay for their sins) is more important than acting in love.
- The resolution to this conundrum (in my mind) is to believe that God does not have unlimited power. That is, God cannot simply intervene in history or beyond history to dictate what happens. To put it bluntly, if God has the power to end suffering as a singular act, but does not do so, then God is not "pure, unbounded love." This reduced dimension of power is not a matter of God's self-limitation. God does not choose to restrict the exercise of divine power. God's power is limited by God's own nature.
- In this way of thinking, God's power is the power of invitation. God is present in each moment, offering the highest possibilities for love and justice (understanding "justice" as the social form of love). We choose whether or not to accept God's invitations. When we say yes, we enter a partnership with God to live toward the world of love that God seeks for all. When we do not accept that invitation, we are left with lesser possibilities.
- This process goes on throughout every life and every moment of history. It is not a matter of things getting better every day in every way. Some days we welcome God's invitations and experience the fulfillment that comes with a sense of partnership with God, whereas on other days we reject those invitations, and the consequences fall to us.
- From this point of view, one of the great things about God, as one of my colleagues says, is that God never gives up. No matter how often we refuse and even subvert the invitations from the divine, God continues unrelentingly to offer possibilities for good from day to day, hour to hour, moment by moment, and even breath by breath.

In this framework (and in the Bible itself) love is less a feeling and more an action intended to be for the good of the individual, the human community, and the world itself.

The question of accountability does come up. As several people in Bible studies over the years have asked, "Do you believe that people who do evil things get off scot-free?" "Is there no punishment?" Here an adaptation of a Jewish way of thinking that is taken up in the New Testament makes sense to me. In the midst of a reflection on God punishing God's enemies, the Wisdom of Solomon observes that when the people of Israel worshiped "irrational serpents and worthless animals," God punished them by sending "a multitude of irrational creatures . . . , so that they might learn that *one is punished by the very things by which one sins*" (Wis 11:15–16; italics added). In Romans 1:24–32, Paul uses a similar notion, lamenting that the gentiles had worshiped idols and consequently, God "gave them over" to suffer the sins that befall idolaters. A similar idea surfaces in Revelation 13:10: "If you kill with the sword, with the sword you must be killed." While I do not join the writer of Wisdom or Paul in thinking that God initiates punishment, my demythologizing mind believes that when we sin, the act of sin creates its own punishment in that we deny ourselves the fulfillment that comes from living according to God's purposes. God does not actively bring about retribution. We punish ourselves. In the strict sense, we create our own hells as we suffer the logical outcomes of violating God's desires.

To be sure, the consequences of disobedience are not always immediate. Indeed, they can take generations. Paul anticipated that the second coming and the collapse of the Roman Empire would take place shortly after his writing, but the empire in the West was not defeated until 476 CE. Moreover, when we build our worlds on false values—such as worshiping things like power, money, race, class, and nation—those behaviors create personal and social tensions that deny individuals, households, and communities the quality of life that is possible when we accept God's invitations toward the good—a world of love, justice, peace, dignity, freedom, and abundance. And, I have to admit, the consequences of violation are sometimes unjustly distributed. The wealthy suffer from living according to false values and experiencing social and personal tensions that come from the current global economic system and its exploitation and reliance on violence, but the wealthy suffer in much greater comfort than the billions of impoverished who live from day to day and are ground down by racism.

With respect to what happens in the afterlife, I admit to being agnostic. This hesitance applies to both punishment and blessing. I do not *know* whether some form of hell or heaven lies ahead. Yes, I recognize that our conscious awareness is limited. More is going on in this life than we can describe scientifically. Much of our apprehension is intuitive and takes place at levels of feeling. I have a sense of a "more" in the present, and it seems possible—even logical—to me that there could be something "more" in an afterlife.

As a process theologian, the view of the afterlife sketched in chapter 11 is attractive. It proposes a next life of consciousness being alive in the consciousness of God and thus being aware of other consciousnesses. In a manner with a family resemblance to purgation, this view also makes accountability explicit. In the freedom that comes from becoming conscious in the consciousness of the mind of God, we become fully aware of how our lives have affected others, including the ways we have harmed others, and we understand the depth of violation that we have perpetrated. In a sense, we experience their experience of violation. What a stunning indictment. This is a moment of hell that I have created for myself.

But the unrelenting love of God is truly unrelenting and does not leave us stuck in that moment but acts for the good by releasing us from being imprisoned in that moment of indictment. As Marjorie Suchocki hypothesizes, "What is happening in the very process of judgment is that the ego is being opened up to that which is more than itself. The participation in the other through the power of God is not only judgment. It is the route to transformation of justice. . . . [The participants] move from a knowledge of [themselves] . . . to a knowledge of [themselves] in God." And "the ultimate transformation and unity in God is love, pervasive, deep, everlasting."[2] The consciousness of gracious love embraces our consciousness. But I do not *know* that such things occur.

With respect to the possibility of a next life, the bottom line for me is this: I believe that the God in whom I have trusted in this life—and who always proves faithful to be present, ever supportive, and always inviting toward the good—is a God whom I can trust for the future. In the same way that I have not known the particulars of how my life would unfold in the present, I have always found God faithful. While I do not have the particulars of a possible life beyond, my experience joins those who sing, "God has not failed me yet." I can trust that.

What Does Bob Believe?

I (Bob) was born and raised, until midway through my high school years, in the Episcopal Church. During those early years of life, I was very active in church life, but I don't remember spending much time thinking about hell. We recited the creeds, both Apostles' and Nicene, which mention divine judgment and, in the case of the Apostles' Creed, Christ's descent into the realm of the dead (Hades). While my time in the Episcopal Church didn't lead to deep thinking about hell, during high school I began attending a Bible study sponsored by the local Foursquare Gospel Church, a church I later joined. During this period I was introduced to the idea that hell was the destination of those who did not believe in Jesus. My view of who might make it into heaven became rather limited. I wasn't even sure about members of other churches that weren't as "biblically based" as mine. Perhaps the people in those churches who weren't as zealous as those of us in my group might not make it to heaven and would spend eternity in hell. To be honest, I wasn't sure about myself. I also began to read about what were considered unorthodox religious groups like the Jehovah's Witnesses, who taught a form of annihilationism. The books I was reading suggested that to cease to exist was worse than suffering fiery torment in hell for eternity. During this fundamentalist season of my life, I became fully invested in the idea that human sin was so egregious that God was right to sentence anyone who failed to believe in Jesus to eternal damnation.

I no longer embrace that view of divine judgment or the view of God's nature that undergirds it. Over time, beginning in college and then more fully in seminary, I began to question what

I had been taught about judgment and hell. I encountered other thinkers, especially during seminary, that opened my perspectives on things, thinkers that included Karl Barth, Dietrich Bonhoeffer, Hans Küng, and especially Jürgen Moltmann. I wasn't ready to embrace universalism, but I began to question the idea that a loving God might sentence a person to an eternity of torment.

My first stop on the journey to where I stand today came in seminary when I was reintroduced to the idea of annihilation. Believing still that confession of faith in Christ was a necessary part of the process of salvation, but not willing to consign most of the world to eternal torment, I embraced what is known as conditionalism or annihilationism. I learned that leading evangelicals such as John Stott, and my teacher, Colin Brown, embraced this idea. Annihilation made sense for several reasons. It removed the threat of eternal torment. It also seemed to fit with my embrace of conditional immortality. If humans did not have an immortal soul, then on what basis would they gain access to the afterlife, unless God sustained them in that state of being? Finally, the idea of annihilationism seemed to make space for the working out of God's justice. Reading Scripture, I encountered passages that spoke of the fire of judgment. While Augustine might offer a way for bodies to withstand the fire so they can experience eternal torment, I came to believe that fire consumes. I held that view for many years because the question that stayed with me during this period had to do with Paul's words about the wages of sin leading to death (Rom 6:23), as well as the passages that spoke of divine judgment, including the parable of the Sheep and Goats in Matthew 25.

However, the second half of that verse from Romans 6 raised a different question. What does it mean when Paul writes that "the free gift of God is eternal life in Christ Jesus our Lord"? Even though I couldn't reconcile a loving and merciful God with a God who sentenced humans to an eternity of torment, one reason I stayed with some form of punishment, even if it was eternal death, was to make sense of the fate of people like Hitler, Stalin, and Pol Pot of the killing fields of Cambodia. If people like them didn't face some form of justice in life, shouldn't they face justice in the afterlife? If there is not some form of punishment on the other side of the grave, how might God's vengeance be taken on them? Is this not the message we hear from Paul when he writes to the church in Rome, "Beloved, never avenge yourselves, but leave room for the wrath of God, for it is written, 'Vengeance is mine; I will repay, says the Lord'" (Rom 12:19; cf. Deut 32:35–36)? Isn't this a concept that sustained early Christians as they endured persecution? My reading of Paul led me to believe that he didn't embrace eternal punishment, but rather taught that the fate of the wicked or unbeliever is death or annihilation. This was in keeping with early Jewish thinking.

As you will have discovered in reading the historical sections of this book, Christians have embraced many perspectives on divine judgment, eternal punishment, and salvation itself. Some thinkers, including Origen and Gregory of Nyssa, envisioned the possibility that in the end, God would reconcile everyone and everything, so that even if there was a time of purgation after death in something akin to hell, eventually everyone would be reunited with God, and hell would cease to exist. That idea makes sense to me because it has biblical and historical support.

As I have tried to make sense of what the future holds, whether heaven or hell exists beyond the grave, I have also sought to keep in place the tension between the justice of God and the love of God; I try to keep in mind the problem of evil in this world, and the ease with which I can dispense with the idea of God's wrath when I live in a comfortable, middle-class, suburban reality. It's not so easy to dispense with it when you experience oppression and lose hope that justice will be served in life.

If vengeance belongs to God, as Deuteronomy and Paul suggest (Deut 32:35–36; Rom 12:19), then how does that take place? Resolving the problem of hell is not easy. Nevertheless, mindful of why others might think differently, I have chosen to emphasize God's love over God's justice. I have found a sense of hope that God will, in Christ, reconcile all things, and that my calling is to serve as an ambassador of that promise (2 Cor 5:16–21). In my estimation, that involves the restoration of all things, such that evil will be no more, and God will be "all in all" (1 Cor 15:28).

So how did I get to where I am now? Some of the influences come from theologians like Barth and Moltmann, as well as my more recent engagement with Orthodox thinkers. Perhaps the keystone for my movement toward an inclusive vision of the future is rooted in friendships that developed over the past several decades with people who follow religious traditions different from my own—Judaism, Islam, Hinduism, and others. While my core theological position might be found within what is known as the inclusivist position, such that we are all eventually reconciled to God through Christ, I no longer feel compelled to convert my friends to my faith so they can experience reconciliation with God. I expect my Jewish, Hindu, and Muslim friends may feel the same about me. It's not that all roads lead to the same place, but that in the end, we will be one with God. If so, that leaves little room for hell. I don't think it leaves much room for annihilation. However, one challenge to my universalist perspective is the role of human freedom. Could it be that some will refuse the offer of friendship with God? Even then I can envision God being persistent in reclaiming every one of us. Why does death have to be the endpoint for God's reach? Again, we may need to spend some time in God's refining fire, so that as Moltmann writes of God's refining fire, "it is an image for God's love, which burns away everything which is contrary to God so that the person whom God has created will be saved."[3] Perhaps the fire spoken of in Scripture might be a refining element rather than a punishing one.

So today I no longer believe in hell or annihilation. Instead, I embrace the wideness of God's mercy, which is wider than the sea: "For the love of God is broader than the measure of our mind, and the heart of the Eternal is most wonderfully kind."[4] Yes, this is the God who is merciful and loving and who restores all things to God's ultimate vision of reality. What that looks like, I cannot fully describe. But my heart tells me that something is lying beyond the grave, and I hold out hope that it is a physical reality, not just a spiritual one, where body and spirit are reunited in the resurrection of the body. When we find ourselves on the other side of the grave, with our lives fully refined by God's refining fire of judgment, we will be reunited with family and friends. We might meet up with people we've always wanted to meet. But most of all, we will experience the restoration of all things, what some Orthodox theologians have called *apokatastasis,* so that we might fully participate in the life of God. As the late Russian Orthodox theologian Sergius Bulgakov put it, "The power of redemption is unconquerable and irrefusable, as the gift of divinization offered through the incarnation. And in this sense, we can actually equate the redemption with the apocatastasis in its inner essence, as not limited in any way except solely in the form of its accomplishment."[5] The form of its accomplishment lies beyond our line of sight, so whatever we believe about the afterlife and hell specifically is a matter of faith. I know what I believe, but I seek to hold these beliefs lightly and humbly.

Study Guide

As the authors of this book, we believe this study guide will prove valuable for both individual reading and small-group discussions. Therefore, we offer this study guide to help readers and groups effectively utilize our book.

Each participant in the group study should have a copy of the book so they can prepare for the conversation. While not every session focuses on the Bible, having a copy of the Bible is also important, because the Bible comes up even when it is not the focus.

We encourage group leaders to adapt the questions in the guide to their context. It is not necessary to cover every question. We believe that this conversation should be carried out in the context of prayer. Therefore, we encourage the group to begin and end the sessions with prayer. While this study guide offers five sessions, groups may decide to extend the conversation over a longer period or to reduce the conversation to fewer sessions. The book itself is divided into four sections. You may want to divide part 1 (Bible) or part 2 (history) of the study guide into two sessions.

Each session in this series invites readers to think about how they envision the future, whether there will be a day of judgment and some form of punishment (whether eternal or temporary), and why they believe as they do.

- Session 1 focuses on some introductory questions and the biblical materials.

- Session 2 picks up the conversation about divine judgment and the descriptions of hell and its alternatives in the second century and moves forward toward the twentieth century.
- Session 3 focuses on Roman Catholic perspectives.
- Session 4 offers a study of several contemporary options that are more commonly accepted among Protestants, though the chapter on liberation theology includes Roman Catholic contributions. Participants are invited to discuss the various options that tend to be alternatives to the traditional view of hell as the destiny of the damned.
- Session 5 considers the three primary perspectives on divine judgment and hell: eternal torment, conditionalism/annihilationism, and universalism. This session can provide participants an opportunity to discuss their possible landing places when it comes to this issue that troubles so many.

Before turning to the suggestions for study, we make an appeal that should not be necessary in a document related to a Christian community. It is a call for all involved in situations in which reconceived notions of hell become the subject of conversation to relate with one another with patience and respect. The early twenty-first century has become a culture of partisanship and fractionalization in which disrespect, demonizing, and other rude and community-destroying patterns of communication are everyday affairs. Bob and Ron have been part of occasional explorations of hell when some involved have responded to others with considerable verbal lightning and thunder. We have seen and heard Christians ridicule one another. We have witnessed participants talk over others, not even taking the time to listen to what others might actually say. And, yes, we have heard Christians speak as if they have the power to consign others to hell. Indeed, according to at least one person, at death Ron should take with him a firefighter's heavy coat, helmet, and boots as essential garb for where he will spend eternity.

However, until the realm of God comes in its final fullness, all our perceptions have an air of relativity about them. It's a tightrope to walk: we want to believe things that make sense and seem genuinely possible, and yet we should not assume that our preferences are the same as those of God. Those on the rope ought to walk with a little humility.

Study Guide 165

Session One
Introductory Matters and Voices from the Bible

In our previous book, *Second Thoughts about the Second Coming*, we wrote about a theological concept called eschatology, or the study of last things. That includes questions about the afterlife. In this book, we focus more specifically on questions regarding divine judgment and hell.

1. As we begin, here are some questions to help you name your current perceptions and beliefs about hell. These questions set a benchmark for measuring the development of your thoughts across future sessions.

- What is or has been your view of divine judgment and hell? What do you believe coming into this study?
- Why do you believe about hell as you do?
- What has influenced your beliefs on this matter? That is, what are the sources of your beliefs?
- What feelings are evoked by thinking about divine judgment, especially the possibility that you or others might experience hell?
- Does this topic make you feel anxious or hopeful about the future? How does your faith influence your thoughts and feelings on this matter at present?

2. Turning to the Old Testament (chap. 1), we want to explore what these books say about punishment in the afterlife.

- What words does the Bible use to describe the afterlife?
- What do these books say about divine punishment? In this life and in an afterlife?

3. In chapter 2, "Voices from Early Judaism," the authors describe how and when the idea of hell developed.

- Discuss the emergence of this idea, especially the context in which it emerged, and the type of literature that speaks of hell.
- What is the purpose of hell in Jewish thought, whether biblical or extrabiblical?

Beginning with question 4, we move to the New Testament. If you choose to divide this section into two sessions, please begin the new session with a word of prayer. Then review the previous week's conversation before moving into the New Testament questions.

4. The early followers of Jesus who produced the New Testament were influenced by the Old Testament writings and later Jewish writings, especially apocalyptic works like Daniel and 1 Enoch.

– What roles do divine judgment and punishment in the afterlife play in the New Testament writings?
– What is the nature of any punishment that occurs in the afterlife?
– Are there differences of perspective among the New Testament writers?

5. Each of the first three Gospels (Mark, Matthew, and Luke) presents pictures of Jesus' teaching, including thoughts about divine judgment and punishment in the afterlife.

– What do these three Gospels say about divine judgment and hell?
– What are the similarities and differences?
– Did what you find here surprise you, especially in the portrayal of Jesus' teaching on judgment and punishment?
– Luke also wrote a companion volume to his Gospel, the Acts of the Apostles, that describes the expansion of the Jesus movement after the death and resurrection of Jesus. What does this book have to say about hell?

6. The New Testament also includes letters to churches and individuals, offering guidance and direction, and they at times speak of judgment and punishment. The earliest documents in the New Testament are the six accepted Pauline letters. Several letters are attributed to Paul but are considered to be written in Paul's name by followers who sought to extend the apostle's thought to new settings. (This was a commonplace practice in the ancient world.)

– When looking at the acknowledged letters of Paul (Romans, 1 and 2 Corinthians, Galatians, Philippians, and 1 Thessalonians), what do you find about punishment in the afterlife?

– What does Paul say about divine wrath, judgment, and punishment, including the possibility of perishing?

7. Look at the letters that bear Paul's name but are considered post-Pauline (Ephesians, Colossians, 2 Thessalonians, and the Pastoral Epistles).

– What do you find in these letters about punishment in the afterlife?
– Are there differences between these letters and those considered Pauline?

8. We now take up the later letters (James, 1 Peter, Jude, and 2 Peter).

– What are the views expressed here?
– What similarities or differences do you see between these documents and the Pauline letters?

9. The book of Revelation, like the book of Daniel, is an apocalypse.

– How does John of Patmos envision divine wrath, judgment, and punishment of the wicked?
– How do you feel about John's visions of judgment and punishment?
– How do they fit with what you read in the rest of the New Testament?

10. The Johannine literature (Gospel and letters) offers a distinct vision of the future, one that is less apocalyptic than the first three Gospels or Paul and more on the order of realized eschatology.

– What do you find in these texts about judgment and the possibility of consignment to hell?
– How does this view differ from Paul or the first three Gospels?

11. The book of Hebrews is difficult to categorize, but this anonymous document has a message of its own.

– What does this book say about judgment and punishment of the wicked?

- Do you find similarities and differences between Hebrews and the rest of the New Testament?

Session 2
Voices in Christian Tradition

By the early second century, the Christian movement had spread across much of the Roman Empire and probably to Arabia, Persia, and perhaps even to India. It had become increasingly gentile in its makeup. Early Christians took the emerging materials that make up the New Testament, as well as other documents (both Christian and Jewish), to develop their theological positions, which would develop further with time. Church history reveals several theological trajectories, especially as the church divided into Eastern and Western traditions.

While this session covers the entire history of the development of Christian views of judgment and punishment, study groups are invited to divide this session into two parts, with the first session focusing on chapter 4 and the second session focusing on chapter 5, which begins with the Reformation.

1. Distinctive views of divine judgment and punishment in the afterlife developed early in the history of the church.

- What do these early documents—such as Justin Martyr's *First Apology*, the Apocalypse of Peter, as well as the writings of leaders such as Cyprian of Carthage—say about judgment and hell?
- How do they describe hell? How are these portrayals similar to or different from what is found in the New Testament?
- How do the portrayals of judgment and hell look in the years after the Constantinian embrace of Christianity?
- Do they change in any way? Why?

2. Alternatives to the idea of hell as a place of eternal punishment develop in the early church.

- Who are the key individuals who offer alternatives, and where do they hail from, generally?
- What is the nature of their alternatives?

- How do the alternatives differ from the views of the New Testament, especially the first three Gospels and Paul?

3. While Origen and his theological descendants offered one path of thinking, Western Christianity was influenced to a great degree by Augustine of Hippo.

- What did Augustine believe and teach about divine judgment and punishment of the wicked?
- Why did he offer this particular perspective?
- How do Augustine's views influence the ongoing development of the idea of hell in the Western church?

4. Augustine set the table for the primary future developments within the medieval church.

- Who are the key figures in the medieval church? How do they build on and further develop the ideas of Augustine regarding judgment and hell?

5. Some interpreters say that Dante Alighieri influenced popular views of hell that remain influential today.

- What are Dante's views and the legacy of his book *The Divine Comedy*, especially the *Inferno*?
- Do you see influences from earlier writings, such as the Apocalypse of Peter, on his writings? How does he incorporate or develop those ideas?
- To what degree does what many people believe today about hell reflect Dante's views?

Beginning with question 6, we move to chapter 5, which takes the story from the Reformation to the end of the nineteenth century. If you choose to divide this section into two sessions, please begin the new session with a word of prayer. Then review the previous week's conversation before moving on to the next set of questions.

6. The origins of the Reformation of the sixteenth century are linked to Martin Luther, but Erasmus of Rotterdam, a humanist

scholar of the same era who did not leave the Catholic Church, helped influence discussions at the time and in the future.

- What impact did Erasmus have on future developments on the topic of hell?

7. Martin Luther, Ulrich Zwingli, and John Calvin are considered the preeminent voices among the Reformers.

- What did each of these three figures teach on the subject of hell?
- Where did they agree or disagree?
- What are the future implications or impact of their views?

8. Besides the so-called Magisterial Reformers (Luther, Zwingli, and Calvin), there were other movements of reform known collectively as the Anabaptists or Radical Reformers.

- What views did these figures hold?
- How do their views compare and contrast with the Magisterial Reformers?

9. Reform and renewal also took place within the Roman Catholic Church.

- What kinds of developments do we see there, such as with the Jesuits?

10. As the sixteenth century gave way to the seventeenth, the Protestant and Catholic divisions had hardened, and views were more standardized. However, new developments emerged on the topic of hell, which expanded some ideas further and solidified others.

- Focusing on developments in England, what were the views expressed by figures such as Thomas Hobbes and John Bunyan?
- How do they relate to the earlier views of the Reformers? And to future developments?

11. Near the end of the seventeenth century, the Enlightenment—a new intellectual movement that called into question many earlier traditions, especially religious ones—emerged.

Study Guide 171

- Who are some of this era's representative figures? What views did they express on the subject of hell?
- How are the views of these figures different from or similar to earlier views?
- Do you see here developments that have influenced more contemporary views, especially when it comes to matters of authority regarding religion?

12. With the dawn of the nineteenth century we draw closer to the world as we know it. Theological movements, both conservative and liberal, emerged that have continued to influence contemporary thinking. This includes views of divine judgment and the existence of hell.

- Discuss the representative figures of this era and their understandings of divine judgment and hell.
- What trajectories do you see present that relate to contemporary options on these subjects? What are your thoughts and feelings about these developments and trajectories?

13. With the Reformation as your starting point, what trajectories do you see emerging over the three centuries that followed the break of Luther, Zwingli, and others with the Roman Catholic Church?

- What are some of the commonalities and some of the differences?
- Do you see any hints of what might emerge in the twentieth century in these developments?

Session 3
Roman Catholic Voices

Because the Roman Catholic Church has ancient roots and continues to have strong representation across the globe, we are dedicating one session to this tradition. You will notice connections with earlier historical discussions, but this chapter focuses on more recent developments in each of these traditions.

1. Western or Latin Christianity emerged over time, becoming what we know as Roman Catholicism. When it comes to the

question of judgment and hell, Augustine of Hippo provided the foundations for later developments that were expanded by Thomas Aquinas and others, including Dante Alighieri. Modern Catholic doctrine, as expressed in the teachings of Vatican II and the catechism, builds on these earlier developments (see chap. 6).

– How does modern Catholicism define judgment, purgatory, and hell?
– At this point in the study, what do you think of the idea of purgatory?

2. The chapter on Roman Catholic perspectives discusses four key Catholic figures—Joseph Ratzinger (Pope Benedict XVI), Karl Rahner, Hans Urs von Balthasar, and Hans Küng.

– How do each of these theologians view judgment, purgatory, and hell?
– How are they different and similar?

3. Having been introduced to these important figures, along with key documents, how would you describe Roman Catholic understandings?

– Are they monolithic or diverse?
– Do you find any of these perspectives more or less attractive? Why?

Session 4
Voices from the Contemporary World

This session covers five chapters (7–11), each of which focuses on a particular contemporary theological movement that has implications for understanding the concepts of divine judgment and hell. Most of these movements are predominantly Protestant, but there are some overlaps with Roman Catholicism (for example, liberation theology). The questions invite discussion of each movement, with the final question inviting participants to discuss which, if any, best fit a person's own understanding of God's ultimate purposes, and why.

1. Chapter 7 focuses on the voices of those who seek to modernize the conversation about hell, featuring Rudolf Bultmann and Paul Tillich.

- What does Bultmann mean by demythologizing the biblical story?
- With his approach to demythologizing the biblical story, how does Bultmann speak of hell?
- What does Bultmann mean by myth?
- What are the implications for our discussion of hell?

2. Chapter 8 explores the voices of Karl Barth, Emil Brunner, and their postliberal descendants.

- How does Barth understand divine judgment and hell?
- How does Brunner understand divine judgment and hell?
- Where do they agree and where might they disagree?
- Do you find one or the other more convincing? If so, why?
- If you are not drawn to either of these viewpoints, what are the reasons?

3. Chapter 8 also explores postliberal theology that emerged among theologians who were influenced by Barth—Daniel Migliore, Kathryn Tanner, and Joe R. Jones.

- How does each theologian mentioned understand judgment and hell?
- What ideas are distinctive of each one?
- Do you identify with the viewpoints of any of these thinkers?
- If so, what do you find attractive? If not, why not?

4. In chapter 9, the authors take note of the voices of Ernst Käsemann, Jürgen Moltmann, and Wolfhart Pannenberg, each of whom takes a modified apocalyptic but still future-oriented perspective.

- How do each of these figures understand salvation, judgment, and the possibility of hell?
- What are the similarities and differences between them?
- What are the implications of each figure's position?

5. In chapter 10 we turn to liberation theology, which has some similarities to the views expressed by Käsemann and Moltmann but emerged in a different context and has its own diverse perspectives on punishment, especially in relationship to those who oppress others.

- What is the starting point for the various forms of liberation theology when it comes to salvation, judgment, and the possibility of hell?
- If liberation and the search for justice are central to God's ultimate purposes, how does this commitment get reflected in discussions of judgment and hell?
- If your social position is close to that of the oppressed, how do liberation theology's perspectives on punishment strike you?
- If your social position is close to that of the oppressor, how do liberation theology's perspectives on punishment strike you?

6. Chapter 11 explores forms of open and relational theology, including open theism and process theology. As in other theological families, we find diverse streams.

- When it comes to condemnation and hell, what positions do you find among open theists?
- How do you respond to those positions—especially the open theists who say they would like to believe in universalism but cannot? What are their reasons for hesitating?
- When it comes to condemnation and hell, what positions do you find among open and relational theologians (including process theologians)?
- What are the differences and similarities between open theism and relational theologies?
- What are differences and similarities among relational theologies (including process theology)?
- What are the theological bases for the positions taken by these different points of view?
- Which—if any—of these positions do you find inviting? If so, why? If not, what are your second thoughts?

7. We have read about and discussed five different contemporary perspectives, which are largely found among long-established Protestant or Roman Catholic traditions.

- What is your sense, your feelings, about these different perspectives?
- Now that you have had a chance to consider them all, are there one or more of these perspectives that resonate with you more than the others? If so, why?

Session 5
Three Viewpoints: Eternal Punishment, Annihilationism (Conditionalism), and Universalism

Having explored biblical, historical, and contemporary perspectives on the Last Judgment and hell, in this session we lay out the three basic options for judgment that are prominent in contemporary conversation: eternal punishment, conditionalism, and universalism. These are discussed in chapters 12 through 14.

1. Chapter 12 summarizes the basic tenets of the traditional perspective that the wicked and unbelievers will experience eternal punishment in hell. The chapter points to two ways of conceiving of this punishment—one envisions a person literally burning in hell's fire and the other envisions eternal punishment, but not in fire. Sketch the characteristics of each idea.

- What arguments are given in support of the idea of eternal punishment, whether by fire or in some other way?
- While the modes of punishment might differ, their purpose and duration are the same. What critiques challenge the idea of eternal punishment?
- What are your feelings and thoughts about this position?

2. Annihilationism or conditionalism is an alternative to the traditional belief in hell as eternal punishment (chap. 13).

- How is annihilationism or conditionalism defined?
- What are the arguments offered in support of this position?
- What critiques challenge this perspective?
- What are your feelings and thoughts about this position?

3. Universalism is another alternative view that has been embraced by some Christians since at least the beginning of the third century with Origen and others (chaps. 4 and 14).

- What is the universalist position on hell?
- What are the arguments in support of it?
- What are the critiques of this position?
- What are your feelings and thoughts about this alternative?

4. Having explored three different perspectives on the Last Judgment and the idea of hell as the eternal destiny of some, compare and contrast the three positions.

- What are their strengths and weaknesses?
- Do you find one of these more compelling? Why or why not?

5. In the afterword, the two authors, Bob and Ron, agree on many things, but each has his own perspective on these matters.

- What did they reveal about their views?
- Do you see their views reflecting developments from the earlier discussions in the book?
- What is your reaction to each of their statements?
- What would you like to say to each one?

6. As you conclude this study, consider these questions.

- What have you discovered or rediscovered about how judgment and hell are understood in the Bible and Christian history?
- Did you find anything here, especially in the more contemporary options, that resonates with you? Why is that?

7. In the introduction, we suggest a two-step process for thinking about what you believe about hell: (1) clarifying what the options are, and (2) evaluating the options in light of your deepest convictions about God and God's ultimate purposes. Working through the book has unfolded several possibilities for thinking about hell. In addition, possibilities may have come to you that are not discussed here.

- Which one(s) are closer to and farther from your deepest convictions about God and what God wants for life?

- In light of what you think is most consistent with your vision of God, which possibility in the book or from elsewhere is one with which you can live?
- Has your mind changed in any way? If so, what has changed? How do you feel about this?
- As a final thought, what are the implications of your view of hell for how you think about your own life and the lives of those close to you, implications for how you understand the purpose of the church, and implications for the world?

A Final Word

We hope that these sessions have opened new conversations and perhaps answered questions that have been on one's heart and mind. Our goal has been to inform, and while we have tried to be fair and honest, we hope we have persuaded you to dive deeper into these questions for the good of the world we inhabit.

Notes

Introduction
1. C. S. Lewis, *The Great Divorce: A Dream* (HarperOne, 2001), 140–41.
2. Alan E. Bernstein, *The Formation of Hell: Death and Retribution in the Ancient and Early Christian Worlds* (Cornell University Press, 1993), 3.

Chapter 1: Voices from the Old Testament
1. Clark M. Williamson, *Way of Blessing/Way of Life: A Christian Theology* (ChalicePress, 1999), 16.
2. David Penchansky, "Retribution," in *The New Interpreter's Dictionary of the Bible,* vol. 4, ed. Leander E. Keck et al. (Abingdon Press, 2009), 781.
3. Patrick D. Miller Jr., *Sin and Judgment in the Prophets: A Stylistic and Theological Analysis,* Society of Biblical Literature Monograph Series 27 (Scholars Press, 1982), 1.
4. Miller, *Sin and Judgment,* 5.

Chapter 2: Voices from Early Judaism
1. Quotations from the Apocrypha and Pseudepigrapha are taken from James Charlesworth, ed., *The Old Testament Pseudepigrapha* (Doubleday and Co., 1983).

Chapter 3: Voices from the New Testament
1. See Robert D. Cornwall, *Marriage in Interesting Times: A Participatory Study Guide* (Energion Publications, 2016).
2. Stanley Stowers, *A Rereading of Romans: Justice, Jews, and Gentiles* (Yale University Press, 1994), 105–6.
3. Paul Achtmeier catalogs many nuances of the traditional and contemporary interpretations in his *I Peter,* Hermeneia (Fortress, 1996), 252–63.
4. John H. Elliott, *1 Peter,* Anchor Bible Commentary (Doubleday, 2000), 733–34.

Chapter 4: Voices from the Second Century CE to the Reformation

1. "The Martyrdom of Polycarp, Bishop of Smyrna, as Told in the Letter of the Church of Smyrna to the Church of Philomelium," in *Early Christian Fathers*, ed. Cyril C. Richardson, The Library of Christian Classics (Touchstone, 1996), 153.

2. Justin Martyr, *First Apology of Justin Martyr*, in Richardson, *Early Christian Fathers*, 254, 271.

3. From the Akhmim Fragment of the Gospel of Peter, in *The Apocryphal New Testament*, ed. M. R. James (Clarendon Press, 1924), as found at Early Christian Writings, http://www.earlychristianwritings.com/text/apocalypsepeter-mrjames.html.

4. Cyprian, *To the People of Thibaris, Exhorting to Martyrdom*, Christian Classics Ethereal Library, https://ccel.org/ccel/cyprian/epistles/anf05.iv.iv.lv.html.

5. Cyprian, *An Address to Demetrianus*, Christian Classics Ethereal Library, https://ccel.org/ccel/cyprian/epistles/anf05.iv.v.v.html.

6. Bart D. Ehrman, *Heaven and Hell: A History of the Afterlife* (Simon & Schuster, 2021), 261–64.

7. Bart D. Ehrman, *Journeys to Heaven and Hell: Tours of the Afterlife in the Early Christian Tradition* (Yale University Press, 2022), 91.

8. Alan E. Bernstein, *The Formation of Hell: Death and Retribution in the Ancient and Early Christian Worlds* (Cornell University Press, 1993), 192–93.

9. Bernstein, *Formation of Hell*, 308–11.

10. Origen, *Contra Celsum*, New Advent, https://www.newadvent.org/fathers/04162.htm.

11. Origen, *Contra Celsum*, New Advent, https://www.newadvent.org/fathers/04168.htm.

12. Gregory of Nyssa, *On the Soul and the Resurrection*, Popular Patristics Series, trans. Catharine P. Ross (St. Vladimir's Seminary Press, 1993), 69–73.

13. Gregory of Nyssa, *On the Soul and Resurrection*, 84.

14. John Chrysostom, *Homily 31 on Romans*, New Advent, https://www.newadvent.org/fathers/210231.htm.

15. John Chrysostom, *Homily 3 on Philemon*, New Advent, https://www.newadvent.org/fathers/23093.htm.

16. John of Damascus, *Against the Manicheans*, PG 94:1573AB, quoted in "Saint John of Damascus on Hell," Orthodox Christianity: Then and Now, trans. John Sanidopolous, https://www.johnsanidopoulos.com/2013/12/saint-john-of-damascus-on-hell.html.

17. Maximus the Confessor, *St. Maximus the Confessor's Questions and Doubts*, trans. Despina D. Prassas (Northern Illinois University Press, 2010), 53.

18. Brian E. Daley, *The Hope of the Early Church: A Handbook of Patristic Eschatology* (Baker Academic, 2010), 201–2.

19. Isaac of Nineveh (Isaac the Syrian), *"The Second Part," Chapters IV–XLI*, trans. Sebastian Brock (Peeters, 1995), 171–72.

20. Augustine, *The Enchiridion on Faith, Hope, and Love,* ed. Henri Paolucci (Regnery Gateway, 1961), 109, p. 127.
21. Augustine, *Enchiridion* 111, p. 129.
22. Augustine, *Enchiridion* 113, p. 131.
23. Augustine, *The City of God* 21.2; Bernstein, *Formation of Hell,* 318–19.
24. *The Church Teaches: Documents of the Fathers of St. Mary's College* (Tan Books and Publishers, 1973), 345.
25. Gregory the Great, *Moralia,* quoted in Alan E. Bernstein, *Hell and Its Rivals: Death and Retribution among Christians, Jews, and Muslims in the Early Middle Ages* (Cornell University Press, 2017), 55, Kindle. Bernstein devotes chap. 1 of *Hell and Its Rivals* to Gregory's understandings of hell.
26. Hugh of St. Victor, "On the Sacraments of the Christian Faith," in *A Scholastic Miscellany: Anselm to Ockham,* ed. and trans. Eugene R. Fairweather, The Library of Christian Classics (Westminster Press, 1956), 301–2.
27. *Summa theologica, Supplement to the Third Part,* q.69, a.2, New Advent, https://www.newadvent.org/summa/5069.htm.
28. Henry Ansgar Kelly, "Hell with Purgatory and Two Limbos: The Geography and Theology of the Underworld," in *Hell and Its Afterlife: Historical and Contemporary Perspectives,* ed. Isabel Moreira and Margaret Toscano (Ashgate Publishing, 2010), 121, 128.
29. Thomas Aquinas, *Summa theologica, Supplement,* q.99, a.1, a.2, New Advent, https://www.newadvent.org/summa/5099.htm.
30. Thomas Aquinas, *Summa theologica, Supplement,* Appendix II, New Advent, https://www.newadvent.org/summa/7001.htm.
31. Humbert of Romans, *Treatise on the Formation of Preachers,* in *Early Dominicans: Selected Writings,* trans. Simon Tugwell, OP (Paulist Press, 1982), 187–88 (emphasis ours).
32. See Bernstein, *Hell and Its Rivals,* chap. 4, for descriptions of these alternatives, including escapes and rescues.
33. References to *The Inferno* and *The Divine Comedy* are from *The Portable Dante,* ed. and trans. Mark Musa, Penguin Classics (Penguin Books, 1995).
34. Eleonore Stump, "Dante's Hell, Aquinas' Moral Theory, and the Love of God," *Canadian Journal of Philosophy* 16, no. 2 (1986): 195–96.
35. Stump, "Dante's Hell," 197.

Chapter 5: Voices from the Reformation to the Twentieth Century

1. Desiderius Erasmus, *The Praise of Folly,* trans. Clarence H. Miller (Blackmore Dennett, 2018), Kindle.
2. Alice K. Turner, *The History of Hell* (Harcourt Brace, 1993), 160.
3. Martin Luther, "A Sermon on Preparing to Die," in *Martin Luther's Basic Theological Writings,* ed. Timothy F. Lull (Fortress Press, 1989), 644.
4. Ulrich Zwingli, *Exposition of the Faith,* in *Zwingli and Bullinger,* ed. G. W. Bromiley, The Library of Christian Classics (Westminster Press, 1953), 254.

5. John Calvin, *Institutes of the Christian Religion in Two Volumes*, ed. John T. McNeill, trans. Ford Lewis Battles, The Library of Christian Classics (Westminster Press, 1960). Locations in the *Institutes* are given in the text.

6. Turner, *History of Hell*, 160.

7. Menno Simons, "Epistle to Micron," in *The Complete Writings of Menno Simons, 1496–1561*, ed. C. Wenger, trans. Leonard Verduin (Herald Press, 1956), 921.

8. See Morwenna Ludlow, "Why Was Hans Denck Thought to Be a Universalist?," *Journal of Ecclesiastical History* 55, no. 2 (2004), https://doi.org/10.1017/S002204690400990X.

9. Zwingli, *Exposition of the Faith*, 254.

10. Jesuit Fathers of St. Mary's College, *The Church Teaches: Documents of the Church in English Translation* (Tan Books and Publishers, 1973), 352.

11. Turner, *History of Hell*, 173.

12. Ignatius of Loyola, "The Spiritual Exercises," in *Ignatius of Loyola: Spiritual Exercises and Selected Works*, ed. George E. Ganss, SJ, The Classics of Western Spirituality (Paulist Press, 1991), 141–42.

13. Philip C. Almond, *Heaven and Hell in Enlightenment England* (Cambridge University Press, 1994), 48–50.

14. John Bunyan, "A Living Death Shall Feed Upon Them," in *The Penguin Book of Hell*, ed. Scott G. Bruce (Penguin Books, 2018), 194.

15. John Tillotson, "Sermon XXXV: Of the Eternity of Hell Torments," in *The Works of the Most Reverend John Tillotson* (London, 1696), 423. Available at Google Books.

16. Almond, *Heaven and Hell*, 156–57.

17. Alister McGrath, ed., *The Christian Theology Reader* (Blackwell Publishers, 1995), 361–62.

18. John Wesley, "The Great Assize," Sermon 15, March 10, 1758, The Wesley Center Online, http://wesley.nnu.edu/john-wesley/the-sermons-of-john-wesley-1872-edition/sermon-15-the-great-assize/.

19. John Wesley, "Of Hell," Sermon 73, October 10, 1782, The Wesley Center Online, http://wesley.nnu.edu/john-wesley/the-sermons-of-john-wesley-1872-edition/sermon-73-of-hell/.

20. John Wesley, "On Eternity," Sermon 54, *John Wesley: Sermons on Several Occasions*, Christian Classics Ethereal Library, https://www.ccel.org.

21. William Law, *The Spirit of Prayer* (London, 1749), 99, Christian Classics Ethereal Library, http://www.ccel.org/ccel/law/prayer.html. For more on Law and others who give possible evidence of universal salvation in the post-Reformation era, see Robin A. Parry with Ilaria L. E. Ramelli, *A Larger Hope? Universal Salvation from the Reformation to the Nineteenth Century* (Cascade Books, 2019).

22. S. T. Coleridge in Geoffrey Rowell, *Hell and the Victorians: A Study of Nineteenth-Century Theological Controversies concerning Eternal Punishment and the Future Life* (Clarendon Press, 1974), 43.

23. Charles Spurgeon, *Turn or Burn (Annotated)*, ed. Larry Slawson (2019), Kindle Edition, loc. 67 of 305.

24. Charles Spurgeon, "The Sinner's End," December 28, 1862, Spurgeon Center, https://www.spurgeon.org/resource-library/sermons/the-sinners-end/#flipbook/.

25. John Newman, *Apologia pro Vita Sua*, Penguin Classics (Penguin Books, 1994, 2004), Kindle loc. 1025 of 11565.

26. Turner, *History of Hell*, 233–34.

27. Lant Carpenter quoted in Rowell, *Hell and the Victorians*, 43.

28. Rowell, *Hell and the Victorians*, 181.

29. Rowell, *Hell and the Victorians*, 192.

30. Rowell, *Hell and the Victorians*, 205–6.

31. Gary Scott Smith, "Changing Conceptions of Hell in Gilded Age America," *Fides et Historia* 47, no. 1 (2015): 3.

32. Paul Thorsell, "Schleiermacher's Repudiation of Dordrecht in His Essay 'On the Doctrine of Election,'" *International Journal of Systematic Theology* 18, no. 2 (2016): 160–62.

33. Friedrich Schleiermacher, *Christian Faith*, trans. Terrence N. Tice, Catherine L. Kelsey, and Edwina Lawler, ed. Catherine L. Kelsey and Terrence N. Tice, 2 vols. (Westminster John Knox Press, 2016), 1221, Kindle.

34. Schleiermacher, *Christian Faith*, 1548, Kindle.

35. Schleiermacher, *Christian Faith*, 1549–50, Kindle.

36. Rowell, *Hell and the Victorians*, 221.

Chapter 6: Voices from the Roman Catholic Church

1. John F. Clarkson, SJ, et al., *The Church Teaches: Documents of the Church in English Translation* (Tan Books and Publishers, 1973), 352–53.

2. Elmar Klinger, "Purgatory," in *Encyclopedia of Theology: A Concise Sacramentum Mundi*, ed. Karl Rahner (Burnes & Oates, 1975), 1320.

3. Catechism of the Catholic Church 1035, The Holy See, https://www.vatican.va/archive/ENG0015/_P2O.HTM.

4. Cindy Wooden, "Pope Francis Says He Hopes Hell Is 'Empty,'" *America: The Jesuit Review*, January 15, 2024, https://www.americamagazine.org/faith/2024/01/15/pope-francis-resign-interview-246936.

5. Pope Francis, *The Name of God Is Mercy: A Conversation with Andrea Tornielli*, trans. Oonagh Stransky (Random House, 2016), 50.

6. Joseph Ratzinger, *Eschatology: Death and Eternal Life*, 2nd ed., trans. Michael Waldstein (Catholic University of America Press, 1988), 215.

7. Ratzinger, *Eschatology*, 216.

8. Ratzinger, *Eschatology*, 230–31.

9. Karl Rahner, *Foundations of Christian Faith: An Introduction to the Idea of Christianity*, trans. William V. Dych (Crossroad, 1976), 102–3.

10. Karl Rahner, "Hell," in *Encyclopedia of Theology: A Concise Sacramentum Mundi*, 603.

11. Rahner, "Hell," 603–4.
12. Rahner, *Foundations of Christian Faith*, 443.
13. Rahner, "Hell," 604.
14. Rahner, "Hell," 604.
15. Hans Urs von Balthasar, *Dare We Hope: "That All Men be Saved"? With a Discourse on Hell*, trans. David Kipp and Lothar Krauth (Ignatius Press, 2014), 22.
16. Von Balthasar, *Dare We Hope*, 130–31.
17. Von Balthasar, *Dare We Hope*, 142.
18. Von Balthasar, *Dare We Hope*, 149, 176–77.
19. Hans Küng, *Eternal Life? Life after Death as a Medical, Philosophical, and Theological Problem* (Doubleday, 1984), 131.
20. Küng, *Eternal Life?*, 41–42.

Chapter 7: Voices from the Modern Worldview (Bultmann and Tillich)

1. Rudolf Bultmann, "The New Testament and Mythology," in *New Testament and Mythology and Other Basic Writings*, ed. Schubert M. Ogden (Fortress Press, 1984), 1.
2. Bultmann, "New Testament and Mythology," 3.
3. Rudolf Bultmann, *Jesus Christ and Mythology* (Charles Scribner's Sons, 1958), 18.
4. Bultmann, *Jesus Christ and Mythology*, 20.
5. Bultmann, *Jesus Christ and Mythology*, 20.
6. Roger E. Olson, *The Journey of Modern Theology: From Reconstruction to Deconstruction* (IVP, 2013), 331–38.
7. *New World Encyclopedia*, "Rudolf Bultmann," accessed April 13, 2024, https://www.newworldencyclopedia.org/entry/Rudolf_Bultmann.
8. Paul Tillich, *Systematic Theology: Three Volumes in One* (University of Chicago Press, 1971), 1:8, 30–31, 34, 59–65; 2:13–16.
9. Tillich, *Systematic Theology*, 1:49.
10. Tillich, *Systematic Theology*, 1:34–40.
11. Paul Tillich, "You are Accepted," in *The Shaking of the Foundations* (Charles Scribner's Sons, 1948), 155.
12. Tillich, "You Are Accepted," 162.
13. Tillich, *Systematic Theology*, 3:281.
14. Tillich, *Systematic Theology*, 3:418.
15. Tillich, *Systematic Theology*, 3:284.

Chapter 8: Voices Reclaiming Revelation (Barth, Brunner, and the Postliberals)

1. Karl Adam, in *Das Hochland*, June 1926, quoted in John McConnachie, "The Teaching of Karl Barth: A New Positive Movement in German Theology," *Hibbert Journal* 25, no. 3 (1926–27): 385–86.

2. Karl Barth, *Church Dogmatics*, II/2, *The Doctrine of God*, trans. Geoffrey Bromiley (T&T Clark, 1957), 748–49.

3. Barth, *Church Dogmatics*, II/2:752.

4. Karl Barth, "Questions and Answers at the Conference of the World Student Christian Federation in Strasbourg: 1960," in *Barth in Conversation*, ed. Eberhard Busch, vol. 1 (Westminster John Knox Press, 2017), 77.

5. Barth, "Questions and Answers," 75.

6. Barth, "Questions and Answers," 75.

7. Barth, "Questions and Answers," 75.

8. Barth, "Questions and Answers," 76.

9. Karl Barth, *The Humanity of God*, trans. John Newton Thomas (John Knox Press, 1960), 61–62.

10. Karl Barth, "Conversation with Representatives of the YMCA, Südbaden: October 30, 1967," in *Barth in Conversation*, ed. Eberhard Busch, vol. 3 (Westminster John Knox Press, 2019), 275, Kindle.

11. Karl Barth, "Conversation with Methodist Preachers: 1961," in *Barth in Conversation*, 1:130.

12. George Hunsinger, "Hellfire and Damnation: Four Ancient and Modern Views," *Scottish Journal of Theology* 51, no. 4 (1998): 427.

13. Emil Brunner, *Eternal Hope*, trans. Harold Knight (Westminster Press, 1954), 177.

14. Emil Brunner, *The Christian Doctrine of God*, vol. 1 of *Dogmatics*, trans. Olive Wyon (Lutterworth Press, 1949), 52.

15. Brunner, *Eternal Hope*, 84.

16. Brunner, *Christian Doctrine of God*, 320 n. 2.

17. Emil Brunner, *The Christian Doctrine of the Church, Faith, and the Consummation*, vol. 3 of *Dogmatics*, trans. David Cairns (Lutterworth Press, 1962), 418.

18. Emil Brunner, *The Christian Doctrine of Creation and Redemption*, vol. 2 of *Dogmatics*, trans. Olive Wyon (Westminster Press, 1952), 183–84; Jordan Wessling, "How Does a Loving God Punish? On the Unification of God's Love and Punitive Wrath," *International Journal of Systematic Theology* 19 (October 2017): 425.

19. Brunner, *Christian Doctrine of the Church*, 420.

20. Brunner, *Christian Doctrine of the Church*, 424.

21. Sheila Geeve Davaney and Delwin Brown, "Postliberalism," in *The Blackwell Encyclopedia of Modern Christian Thought*, ed. Alister E. McGrath (Blackwell Publishers, 1993), 455.

22. Daniel L. Migliore, *Faith Seeking Understanding: An Introduction to Christian Theology*, 3rd ed. (Eerdmans, 2014), 366, Kindle.

23. Migliore, *Faith Seeking Understanding*, 366–67, Kindle.

24. On the question of divine grace and salvation, see Kathryn Tanner, *Christ the Key* (Cambridge University Press, 2010), chap. 2.

25. Kathryn Tanner, *Jesus, Humanity, and the Trinity: A Brief Systematic Theology* (Fortress Press, 2001), 111.

26. Kathryn Tanner, *Economy of Grace* (Fortress Press, 2005), 1126–27, Kindle.
27. Tanner, *Economy of Grace*, 408–9, Kindle.
28. Tanner, *Economy of Grace*, 1001, Kindle.
29. Joe R. Jones, *A Grammar of Christian Faith: Systematic Explorations in the Christian Life and Doctrine*, vol. 2 (Rowman & Littlefield, 2002), 709–10.
30. Jones, *Grammar of Christian Faith*, 720.
31. Jones, *Grammar of Christian Faith*, 721–22.

Chapter 9: Voices of Eschatological Theologians (Käsemann, Moltmann, and Pannenberg

1. On defining eschatology and apocalyptic theology, see Ronald J. Allen and Robert D. Cornwall, *Second Thoughts about the Second Coming* (Westminster John Knox Press, 2023).
2. Ernst Käsemann, *On Being a Disciple of the Crucified Nazarene*, ed. Rudolph Landau and Wolfgang Kraus, trans. Roy A. Harrisville (Eerdmans, 2010), 11–12.
3. Ernst Käsemann, *Church Conflicts: The Cross, Apocalyptic, and Political Resistance*, ed. Ry O. Siggelkow, trans. Roy A. Harrisville (Baker Academic, 2021), 202.
4. Käsemann, *Church Conflicts*, 213–14.
5. Käsemann, *On Being a Disciple*, 102.
6. Käsemann, *On Being a Disciple*, 314.
7. Jürgen Moltmann, *A Broad Place: An Autobiography*, trans. Margaret Kohl (Fortress Press, 2009), 101.
8. Jürgen Moltmann, *Sun of Righteousness, Arise! God's Future for Humanity and the Earth*, trans. Margaret Kohl (Fortress Press, 2010), 134.
9. Moltmann, *Sun of Righteousness*, 131–35.
10. Moltmann, *Sun of Righteousness*, 137.
11. Moltmann, *Sun of Righteousness*, 141.
12. Moltmann, *Sun of Righteousness*, 142.
13. Jürgen Moltmann, *The Coming of God: Christian Eschatology*, trans. Margaret Kohl (Fortress Press, 2004), 3412–13, Kindle.
14. Moltmann, *The Coming of God*, 3687–88, Kindle.
15. Christoph Schwöbel, "Wolfhart Pannenberg," in *The Modern Theologians: An Introduction to Christian Theology in the Twentieth Century*, ed. David F. Ford (Blackwell, 1997), 201.
16. Wolfhart Pannenberg, *Systematic Theology*, vol. 3, trans. Geoffrey W. Bromiley (Eerdmans, 1998), 611.
17. Pannenberg, *Systematic Theology*, 614.
18. Pannenberg, *Systematic Theology*, 615.
19. Wolfhart Pannenberg, *The Apostles' Creed in the Light of Today's Questions*, trans. Margaret Kohl (Westminster Press, 1972), 91–92.
20. Pannenberg, *Systematic Theology*, 617.
21. Pannenberg, *Apostles' Creed*, 94–95.

Notes 187

Chapter 10: Voices from Liberation Theology

1. Clodovis Boff, "Methodology of the Theology of Liberation," in *Systematic Theology: Perspectives from Liberation Theology*, ed. Jon Sobrino, SJ, and Ignacio Ellacuría (Orbis Books, 1996), 13–14.
2. James H. Evans Jr., *We Have Been Believers: An African American Systematic Theology*, 2nd ed. (Fortress Press, 2012), 4167, Kindle.
3. J. Deotis Roberts, "Black Reflections on Eschatology," in *The Cambridge Companion to Black Theology*, ed. Dwight N. Hopkins and Edward P. Antonio (Cambridge University Press, 2012), 219.
4. Jon Sobrino, SJ, "Central Position of the Reign of God in Liberation Theology," in Sobrino and Ellacuría, *Systematic Theology*, 45.
5. Gustavo Gutiérrez, *The God of Life*, trans. Matthew J. O'Connell (Orbis Books, 1991), 118.
6. Leonardo Boff, *Christianity in a Nutshell*, trans. Philip Berryman (Orbis Books, 2013), 958–60, Kindle.
7. James H. Cone, *A Black Theology of Liberation*, 40th anniv. ed. (Orbis Books, 2011), 117.
8. Gutiérrez, *God of Life*, 102–3.
9. James H. Cone, *God of the Oppressed*, rev. ed. (Orbis Books, 1997), 128–29.
10. Cone, *God of the Oppressed*, 210.
11. Cone, *God of the Oppressed*, 213.
12. Cone, *God of the Oppressed*, 218.
13. Gustavo Gutiérrez, *Essential Writings*, ed. James B. Nickoloff (Orbis Books, 1996), 26–27.
14. Gustavo Gutiérrez, *A Theology of Liberation: History, Politics and Salvation*, trans. Sister Caridad Inda and John Eagleson (Orbis Books, 1973), 168.
15. Gutiérrez, *Theology of Liberation*, 261.
16. Cone, *Black Theology of Liberation*, 129.
17. Gutiérrez, *Theology of Liberation*, 152.
18. José Comblin, "Grace," in Sobrino and Ellacuría, *Systematic Theology*, 207.
19. Cone, *Black Theology of Liberation*, 72.
20. Cone, *Black Theology of Liberation*, 73.
21. Evans, *We Have Been Believers*, 4179, Kindle.

Chapter 11: Voices from Open and Relational Theologies

1. Thomas Jay Oord, *Open and Relational Theology: An Introduction to Life-Changing Ideas* (SacraSage Press, 2021).
2. Clark H. Pinnock, introduction to *Searching for an Adequate God: A Dialogue between Process and Free Will Theists*, ed. John B. Cobb Jr. and Clark H. Pinnock (Eerdmans, 2000), x.
3. Thomas Jay Oord, *The Uncontrolling Love of God: An Open and Relational Account of Providence* (IVP Academic Press, 2015). Our emphasis.
4. Thomas Jay Oord, *God Can't: How to Believe in God and Love after Tragedy, Abuse, and Other Evils* (SacraSage Press, 2019).

5. Clark H. Pinnock, "The Destruction of the Finally Impenitent," *Criswell Theological Review* 4 (1992): 347.

6. Julian of Norwich, *The Revelations of Divine Love* in *Women and Religion,* ed. Elizabeth Clark and Herbert Richardson (Harper & Row, 1977), 11, quoted in Clark M. Williamson, *Way of Blessing/Way of Life: A Christian Theology* (Chalice Press, 1999), 316.

7. Gregory of Nyssa, "Sermon on 1 Corinthians 15:28," in Maurice Wiles and Mark Santer, *Documents in Early Christian Thought* (Cambridge University Press, 1975), 257–59, cited in Williamson, *Way of Blessing,* 317.

8. Origen, *On First Principles,* 3.6.1, 3.6.3–5 (SPCK, 1936), cited in Williamson, *Way of Blessing,* 317.

9. Williamson, *Way of Blessing,* 317, 318.

10. Oord, *God Can't,* 161–62.

11. Oord, *God Can't,* 163–64.

12. Marjorie Suchocki, *In God's Presence: Theological Reflections on Prayer* (Chalice Press, 1996), 62.

13. This process is developed in Marjorie Hewitt Suchocki, *God, Christ, Church: A Practical Guide to Process Theology,* rev. ed. (Crossroad, 1997), 210–16.

14. Suchocki, *God, Christ, Church,* 212.

15. Suchocki, *God, Christ, Church,* 213.

16. Suchocki, *God, Christ, Church,* 214.

17. Suchocki, *God, Christ, Church,* 215.

Chapter 12: Voices on a Literal Hell That Continues Forever

1. John F. Walvoord, "The Literal View," in *Four Views on Hell,* ed. John F. Walvoord, Zachary J. Hayes, and Clark H. Pinnock (Zondervan, 1996), 28.

2. Walvoord, "Literal View," 28.

3. Walvoord, "Literal View," 27.

4. Walvoord, "Literal View," 12.

5. Walvoord, "Literal View," 28.

6. William V. Crockett, "Response to John F. Walvoord," in Walvoord, Hayes, and Pinnock, *Four Views on Hell,* 29–30.

7. Crockett, "Response to Walvoord," 30.

8. William B. Crockett, "The Metaphorical View," in Walvoord, Hayes, and Pinnock, *Four Views on Hell,* 57.

9. J. I. Packer, "The Problem of Eternal Punishment," *Crux* 26 (September 1990): 26.

10. Packer, "Problem of Eternal Punishment," 25.

11. J. I. Packer, *Concise Theology: A Guide to Historic Christian Beliefs* (Tyndale House, 1993), 261–62.

12. Packer, *Concise Theology,* 262.

13. Packer, *Concise Theology,* 262–63.

Chapter 13: Voices on Annihilationism

1. Edward Fudge, *The Fire That Consumes: A Biblical and Historical Study of the Doctrine of Final Punishment*, 3rd ed. (Cascade Books, 2013).
2. Clark Pinnock, "Response to William V. Crockett," in *Four Views on Hell*, ed. John F. Walvoord, Zachary J. Hayes, and Clark H. Pinnock (Zondervan, 1996), 85.
3. Clark Pinnock, "The Conditional View," in Walvoord, Hayes, and Pinnock, *Four Views on Hell*, 140.
4. John Stott, "John Stott's Response to Chapter 6," in David L. Edwards and John R. W. Stott, *Essentials: A Liberal-Evangelical Dialogue* (InterVarsity, 1989), 314.
5. Stott, "Response," 314–15.
6. Pinnock, "Conditional View," 140.
7. Pinnock, "Conditional View," 149.
8. Pinnock, "Conditional View," 151.
9. Stott, "Response," 318.
10. Terrance L. Tiessen, "My Long Journey to Annihilationism," in *A Consuming Passion: Essays on Hell and Immortality in Honor of Edward Fudge*, ed. Christopher M. Date and Ron Highfield (Pickwick Publications, 2015), 18, Kindle.
11. John G. Stackhouse, "Terminal Punishment," in *Four Views on Hell*, 2nd ed., ed. Preston Sprinkle (Zondervan Press, 2016), 61, Google Books.
12. Pinnock, "Conditional View," 154.
13. Chris Loewen, "Engaging Gehenna: Seeing Conditional Immortality through the Eyes of Biblical Imagery," in *Deconstructing Hell*, ed. Chad Bahl (SacraSage Press, 2023), 113.

Chapter 14: Voices on Universal Salvation

1. Robin Parry, "A Universalist View," in *Four Views on Hell*, 2nd ed., ed. Preston Sprinkle (Zondervan Press, 2016), 94, Google Books.
2. On conditional immortality, see chap. 12.
3. On annihilationism, see chap. 13.
4. Parry, "Universalist View," 104.
5. John Hick, *Death and Eternal Life* (Macmillan, 1990), 200.
6. John A. T. Robinson, *In the End, God*, rev. ed. (Collins, 1968), 130.
7. Richard Bauckham, "Universalism: A Historical Survey," *Themelios* 4, no. 2 (1979): 27.
8. David Bentley Hart, *That All Shall Be Saved: Heaven, Hell, and Universal Salvation* (Yale University Press, 2019).
9. Hart, *That All Shall Be Saved*, 47.
10. Hart, *That All Shall Be Saved*, 70–71.
11. Hart, *That All Shall Be Saved*, 164.
12. Hart, *That All Shall Be Saved*, 165.
13. Hart, *That All Shall Be Saved*, 27, 62.
14. Parry, "Universalist View," 119.

Afterword

1. Charles Wesley, "Love Divine, All Loves Excelling," *The Chalice Hymnal* (Chalice Press, 1995), 517.
2. Marjorie Suchocki, *God, Christ, Church: A Practical Guide to Process Theology,* rev. ed. (Crossroad, 1997), 215.
3. Jürgen Moltmann, *Sun of Righteousness, Arise! God's Future for Humanity and the Earth,* trans. Margaret Kohl (Fortress Press, 2010), 137.
4. Frederick W. Faber, "There's a Wideness in God's Mercy," *Chalice Hymnal* (Chalice Press, 1995), 73, stanzas 1, 3.
5. Sergius Bulgakov, *The Sophiology of Death: Essays on Eschatology; Personal, Political, Universal* (Cascade Books, 2021), 103.

Suggestions for Further Reading

*T*his lightly annotated list includes books that help interested readers explore more deeply the specific topic of punishment in hell or purgatory and the broader topic of the afterlife. There are, of course, many, many other books. The list is intended to put forward respectful and thoughtful works from a variety of interpretive perspectives.

Bahl, Chad, ed. *Deconstructing Hell.* SacraSage Press, 2023. Fifteen brief, accessible essays include critical reflection on multiple approaches to the afterlife with emphasis on contemporary expressions. Bob introduces the book with a chapter titled "To Hell and Back: A History of Hell."

Bell, Rob. *Love Wins: A Book about Heaven, Hell, and the Fate of Every Person Who Ever Lived.* HarperOne, 2010. This easy-to-read book sparked an intense and widespread conversation, especially in evangelical circles, with its advocacy of universal salvation.

Bernstein, Alan E. *The Formation of Hell: Death and Retribution in the Ancient and Early Christian Worlds.* Cornell University Press, 1993. Concepts of hell from Greece and Rome through Judaism, the Jesus movement, and early Christianity. Widely regarded as an excellent introduction.

Bronner, Leila Leah. *Journey to Heaven: Exploring Jewish Views of the Afterlife.* Urim Publications, 2011. Basic chronological survey of Jewish perspectives.

Bulgakov, Sergei. *The Sophiology of Death: Essays on Eschatology; Personal, Political, Universal.* Cascade Books, 2021. An Orthodox Christian argument for universal salvation.

Ehrman, Bart D. *Heaven and Hell: A History of the Afterlife.* Simon & Schuster, 2020. This immensely popular author follows developments in history from fear of death through issues of justice and the reasons for resurrection, with attention to Jesus, Paul, and the later writings of the New Testament.

Ellens, J. Harold, ed. *Heaven, Hell, and the Afterlife: Eternity in Judaism, Christianity, and Islam.* Praeger, 2013. Chapters compare and contrast the views of the three religions in the title.

Janney, Rebecca Price. *Who Goes There? A Cultural History of Hell.* Moody Publishers, 2009. Reports popular ideas about hell in the United States from the 1700s to today.

Khalil, Mohammad Hassan. *Islam and the Fate of Others: The Salvation Question.* Oxford University Press, 2012. Khalil offers a valuable look at the way Islamic scholars, especially medieval scholars, have interpreted the Qur'anic teaching on judgment and hell.

Raphael, Simcha Paull. *Jewish Views of the Afterlife.* 3rd ed. Rowman & Littlefield, 2019. Detailed chronological survey of Jewish perspectives.

Rusomji, Nerina. *The Garden and the Fire: Heaven and Hell in Islamic Culture.* Columbia University Press, 2009. An exploration of Islamic understandings of heaven and hell that takes note of cultural implications.

Segal, Alan. *Life after Death: A History of the Afterlife in the Religions of the West.* Doubleday, 2004. Consideration of origins and significance of an afterlife among civilizations around Israel (e.g., Egypt, Mesopotamia, Iran, Greece), with a focus on Judaism and paths through the biblical material to some current views.

Walls, Jerry L. *Heaven, Hell, and Purgatory: A Protestant View of the Cosmic Drama; Rethinking the Things That Matter Most.* Brazos Press, 2015. Lucid consideration of many of the questions posed by notions of heaven, hell, and purgatory, offering interpretations of why thinking about such things is important. Walls has written and edited several other books on hell.

www.ingramcontent.com/pod-product-compliance
Lightning Source LLC
Chambersburg PA
CBHW022057290426
44109CB00014B/1134